Working Toward Strategic Change

MICHAEL G. DOLENCE
DANIEL JAMES ROWLEY
HERMAN D. LUJAN

Working Toward Strategic Change

A Step-by-Step Guide to the Planning Process

JOSSEY-BASS
A Wiley Imprint
www.josseybass.com

Published by Jossey-Bass
A Wiley Imprint
989 Market Street, San Francisco, CA 94103-1741   www.josseybass.com

Jossey-Bass books and products are available through most bookstores. To contact Jossey-Bass directly call our Customer Care Department within the U.S. at (800) 956-7739, outside the U.S. at (317) 572-3986 or fax (317) 572-4002.

Jossey-Bass also publishes its books in a variety of electronic formats. Some content that appears in print may not be available in electronic books.

Interior design by Gene Crofts

Library of Congress Cataloging-in-Publication Data

Dolence, Michael G., date.
 Working toward strategic change : a step-by-step guide to the planning process / Michael G. Dolence, Daniel James Rowley, Herman D. Lujan. — 1st ed.
   p.   cm. — (The Jossey-Bass higher and adult education series)
 Includes bibliographical references and index.
 ISBN 0-7879-0796-0
 1. Education, Higher—United States—Administration—Handbooks, manuals, etc. 2. Strategic planning—United States—Handbooks, manuals, etc. 3. Educational change—United States—Handbooks, manuals, etc. I. Rowley, Daniel James, date. II. Lujan, Herman D. III. Title. IV. Series.
 LB2341.D65 1996
 378.1'07—dc20   96-35692

Printed in the United States of America

FIRST EDITION
PB Printing   10 9 8 7 6 5 4 3

The Jossey-Bass
Higher and Adult Education Series

CONTENTS

PREFACE

Today, many colleges and universities in the United States and around the world are involved in strategic planning. Most of these institutions have come to understand that the world is changing in a rapid and substantive way that affects them more and more each day. The promise of strategic planning is that it helps organizations better understand themselves and the world of which they are a part. It does this by examining who and what the organization is, and by identifying what the organization's capabilities and limitations are. Perhaps more important, however, it does this by discovering and analyzing the environmental context in which it exists, which has the ability to affect the organization one way or another.

In our book *Strategic Change in Colleges and Universities: Planning to Survive and Prosper* (Rowley, Lujan, and Dolence, 1997), we developed the rationale that explains why strategic planning in higher education is essential but also different from the business model most organizations use to conduct their planning process. This workbook develops the basic models we presented in our book and develops a scheme of operation that allows those involved in a college or university's strategic planning to step through the process—from initial meetings to developing a written planning document to conducting periodic reviews—in a manner that ensures that the plan remains vital and up-to-date. In this workbook, we describe how a college's or university's strategic planning committee should conduct a successful planning exercise, and we provide guidelines, suggestions, hints, and actual forms that these committees can use to develop a successful strategic planning process. We do this in a way that allows each campus to customize the process for its own unique circumstances while maintaining an overall regimen that ensures that the final plan will contain all of the elements necessary to be effective.

We do not suggest that this manual is a substitute for a professional strategic planning consultant or facilitation support service, which many organizational planning exercises require. In a manual such as this, we cannot anticipate the human dynamics that will be present in each planning scenario, and often circumstances do require professional help. However, we do present a scheme for conducting a strategic planning process that most college and university planning groups will find helpful and informative as they work to develop the most effective strategic plan possible for their campus.

Audience

This workbook is designed to be an effective tool for anyone engaged in strategic planning at any level in a college or university. It is written most directly for the institutional strategic planning committee, but it can work equally well at the college, unit, or even departmental level. It is also designed to be a tool that strategic planning consultants and facilitators can use to help guide the planning committees they work with through this exciting and challenging process.

This workbook is not a substitute for our book *Strategic Change in Colleges and Universities* but rather a series of application tools that follow the general themes and directions of the book. When this workbook does not provide adequate explanation for why a certain step may be important or necessary, we recommend that readers review the information on that topic provided in the book. For example, since our method of strategic planning is not mission-based, participants who question this approach should read the related discussion in the book to understand why we have chosen the methods we have rather than other methods. The book and the workbook are designed to complement rather than replicate each other.

We recommend that each member of the planning committee have a copy of this workbook, as well as a copy of the book. The workbook contains both individual and group exercises and worksheets, and as individual participants work through the material, they will find it useful to refer back to the examples and instructions given for each step. All of the instructions for the use of this workbook are contained within this volume—there is no additional "facilitator's manual" that might supply information not provided here.

The workbook could also be used as a teaching tool by instructors of strategic planning classes to help their students simulate a strategic planning exercise in a hypothetical college or university, or even a nonprofit or governmental organization. Used in such a way it will provide participants with a chance to more closely examine the challenges and opportunities in such organizations in a very realistic and effective manner.

Methods the Workbook Employs

A variety of tools are provided in this workbook. The group process and application tools—both those located at the back of the book and those used in the exercises at the end of each step—can be used by the decision-making committee to make their activities more effective and streamlined. The tools encompass a variety of methods. First, the forms located at the end of each step provide the basic explanation of the exercises, and examples for groups to follow. We have designed the forms and the exercises to allow planning groups to use them as appropriate to do their entire planning process. Second, strategic planning groups may conduct the process using one of the electronic decision support centers that several colleges and universities own or have access to. The trained staff of these centers can facilitate the exercises greatly by taking over much of the work of organizing, prioritizing, and analyzing data sets. Third, the planning committee can employ the method we describe for using spreadsheet templates that are available from the authors for an additional charge. The method simulates many of the decision support center tools, but involves more data manipulation than is usually the case in a decision support center. Nonetheless, it is an easy way to gather, sort, prioritize, and analyze data, and has clear advantages over using paper forms. (We do not suggest that any one method is better than another; we support all three methods to allow each campus maximum flexibility in conducting its own strategic planning process.)

Organization of the Workbook

The organization of this workbook follows the strategic planning engine model introduced in our book. The model contains ten steps, from inception of the plan through the activities of review and revision after a strategic planning committee has completed its planning exercise and written a document. Following a general introduction, which describes a process model that helps strategic planning committees gain a better understanding of the logistics and processes they will be involved with as they go through the strategic planning process, each chapter in the workbook treats a step of the strategic planning engine model as follows: it explains the central purpose of the step, describes what the step is all about, discusses what the results of the step should be for the planning group, offers some hints based on our experiences in working with these materials, and presents a set of reproducible forms or exercises that walk the strategic planning group through the step.

A final note: participants should not consider the steps we present here as necessarily linear in nature. For example, if a campus has already done a substantive internal and external environmental audit, the strategic planning committee can skip Steps 2 and 3, and instead use the results of Step 1 and the data from the environmental studies and go right to Step 4. Likewise, if a college or university has already developed a comprehensive set of goals and objectives, Step 1 should be modified and the group could skip Step 7. In other words, be sure to use the data the campus already has on hand rather than reinventing the proverbial wheel. Where it is possible to reduce the work required to complete the model, the committee should strive to do so. This effort should make adapting this model to individual campuses much easier, and will also respect the work done by others by incorporating it into the strategic planning process. Table P.1 can be used to evaluate where your particular strategic planning group is in the process of developing the items needed to conduct an effective strategic planning process. Go through the table to determine where your group should start (or pick up) the process given the items you may or may not have available to you already.

Table P.1. Take an Inventory.

Read this key completely before beginning the process. Then assemble all of the existing components for review as you assess what you need to do to implement the entire process.

Assess Key Performance Indicators

Do you have key performance indicators (KPIs), objectives (MBOs), critical success factors, etc.? **Note to practitioners**: *KPIs need to be well defined and unambiguous. We suggest assembling them into a catalogue as you develop them.*	IF YOU DO	Use in Step 1 of the strategic planning engine. Proceed to Step 2. You must have KPIs or their equivalent to begin, but you can start the process in a number of places.
	IF YOU DO NOT	Gather using brainstorming or source material. Define each in unambiguous terms. Refine and stratify into primary, secondary, etc. Proceed to Step 2.

External Environmental Assessment

Have you conducted an environmental scan in the past two years (2A)?	IF YOU HAVE	Perform a cross-impact analysis with the results using the KPIs from Step 1 (2D).
	IF YOU HAVE NOT	For each KPI in Step 1, ask what in the environment will help or hinder achievement of the KPI.
Do you have a list of collaborators (shareholders, stakeholders) and the KPIs related to them (2B)?	IF YOU HAVE LIST *AND* KPIs	Perform a cross-impact analysis with your KPIs (2D).
	IF YOU HAVE LIST *OR* KPIs	Brainstorm a list of shareholders and stakeholders or a list of KPIs for either or both—whatever is missing.
	IF YOU HAVE NEITHER	Brainstorm a list of shareholders and stakeholders, and KPIs for each list.
Do you have a list of competitors and their KPIs?	IF YOU HAVE LIST *AND* KPIs	Perform a cross-impact analysis with your KPIs (2D).
	IF YOU HAVE LIST *OR* KPIs	Brainstorm a list of competitors or a list of KPIs—whatever is missing.
	IF YOU HAVE NEITHER	Brainstorm a list of competitors and KPIs.
Do you have a list of opportunities and threats (2E)?	IF YOU DO	Go directly to KSWOT/cross-impact analysis (Step 3).
Note to practitioners: *If you have performed the cross-impact analysis in Steps 2A, 2B, and 2C, it is not necessary to perform the KSWOT cross-impact analysis again in Step 4.*	IF YOU DO NOT	Return to Step 2A, then 2B, and then 2C.

Table P.1. *continued*

Assess the Internal Environment

Do you have an analysis of current performance (3A)? **Note to practitioners**: *You can have a significant impact on KPIs by creatively using organizational structure and functional strategies (i.e., teams, task forces, etc.).*	IF YOU DO	Perform a cross-impact analysis with the results, using the KPIs from Step 1.
	IF YOU DO NOT	At a minimum, develop a list of policies and procedures. For each policy and procedure ask, "Does it help or hinder achievement of each desired KPI in Step 1?" Rate the impact on the 0–6 scale described in the workbook.
Do you have a description of organizational structures and responsibilities (3B)? **Note to practitioner**: *You can have a significant impact on KPIs by creatively using organizational structure and function strategies (i.e. teams, task forces, etc.).*	IF YOU DO	Perform a cross-impact analysis with the results using the KPIs from Step 1.
	IF YOU DO NOT	Document the organizational structure, decision-making process, and functional responsibilities, then ask, "Does each help or hinder achievement of each desired KPI in Step 1?" Rate the impact on the 0–6 scale.
Do you have a list of current strategies, goals, and objectives (3C)?	IF YOU DO Option 1	Perform a cross-impact analysis with the results, using the KPIs from Step 1 to close out the last strategic planning cycle (see Step 10)
	Option 2	Perform a cross-impact analysis with the results using the KPIs from Step 3C to commence the new strategic planning cycle.
	IF YOU DO NOT Option 1	Skip this step, list the lack of formal strategies, goals, and objectives as a general weakness of the institution and proceed to Step 4.
	Option 2	Quickly brainstorm what you believe to be your current strategies, goals, and objectives and perform a cross-impact analysis with the results, using the KPIs.
Do you have a list of strengths and weaknesses (3E)? **Note to Practitioners:** *If you have performed a cross-impact analysis in Steps 3A, 3B, and 3C, it is not necessary to perform the KSWOT cross-impact analysis again in Step 4.*	IF YOU DO	Go directly to KSWOT/cross-impact analysis (Step 4).
	IF YOU DO NOT	Return to Step 3A, then 3B, and then 3C.

Assess the SWOT Analysis

Do you have a list of strengths, weaknesses, opportunities, and threats (SWOTs) from a previous SWOT analysis?	IF YOU DO	Go directly to KSWOT/cross-impact analysis (Step 4).
	IF YOU DO NOT	Go to Step 2A, then 2B, then 2C, and then proceed to Step 3A, then 3B, and then 3C.

Table P.1. *continued*

Assessing Ideas That Work

Do you have a list of ideas?	IF YOU DO	Go directly to KPIs/ideas cross-impact analysis (Step 6).
	IF YOU DO NOT	Brainstorm ideas that make the strengths stronger and the weaknesses weaker; take advantage of opportunities; and mitigate against threats.

KPI/Ideas Cross-Impact Analysis

Do you now have a list of ideas?	IF YOU DO	Perform a cross-impact analysis with the results of the previous step using the KPIs (Step 6).
	IF YOU DO NOT	Return to Step 5.

Synthesizing Strategies, Goals, and Objectives

Do you have new or revised mission, strategies, goals, and objectives?	IF YOU DO	Go directly to KSGO cross-impact analysis. Perform the cross-impact analysis with these items using the KPIs (Step 8).
	IF YOU DO NOT	Go to the next box.
Do you have a list of ideas that are designed to make your strengths stronger and your weaknesses weaker, to take advantage of opportunities, and to mitigate against threats?	IF YOU DO	Cluster the ideas into logical strategic groupings. Articulate the resulting strategies. Evaluate and reformulate the mission statement if necessary. Develop goals and milestones. Develop yearly objectives. Go to KSGO cross-impact analysis (Step 8).
	IF YOU DO NOT	Return to Step 5.

KSGO Cross-Impact Analysis

Do you have a list of the following: ideas clustered into logical strategic groups, articulated resulting strategies, a reevaluated mission statement, developed goals and milestones, and developed yearly objectives?	IF YOU DO	Perform a cross-impact analysis with these several lists using the KPIs (Step 8).
	IF YOU DO NOT	Return to Step 5 or 7, as appropriate.

Implementation Concerns

Do you have a list of the following: ideas clustered into logical strategic groups, articulated resulting strategies, a reevaluated mission statement, developed goals and milestones, and developed yearly objectives?	IF YOU DO	Implement Step 9 and track performance using a quarterly evaluation as described in the workbook.
	IF YOU DO NOT	Return to Steps 5, 6, or 7, as appropriate.

THE AUTHORS

MICHAEL G. DOLENCE is president of Michael G. Dolence and Associates. Formerly he served as strategic planning administrator for the California State University, Los Angeles; director of research, planning, and policy analysis for the Commission on Independent Colleges and Universities; founding director of the New York State Public Opinion Poll; and founding director of the Science, Engineering, and Research Campus Hook-up. While serving as strategic planning administrator at California State University, Dolence had the opportunity to implement a campuswide strategic planning process and to guide the development of an integrated planning and budgeting system.

Dolence consults nationally with higher education institutions, systems, associations, and vendors. He has worked with numerous institutions of higher education to develop campuswide strategic planning processes and strategic enrollment management programs with a special emphasis on crisis avoidance and intervention, and has had extensive experience in developing the tactical plans necessary to implement a strategic management system in a university of 22,000 students. His counsel is sought on strategies for responding to state and federal initiatives, as well as strategies for repositioning institutions for competitiveness. He has also worked with information system vendors in the development of state-of-the-art strategic enrollment and instructional management systems.

Dolence is a specialist in and nationally acclaimed keynote speaker on organizational transformation, strategic positioning, institutional strategic planning and management processes, and strategic enrollment management; in information technology planning and management linking planning and budgeting and linking academic planning and transformation; and in public advocacy and public relations. He has made many presentations before such national audiences as the Society for College and University Planning (SCUP), the American Association of Collegiate Registrars and Admissions Officers, the American Association for Higher Education, the College and University Systems Exchange, and the Interuniversity Communications Council. He is the author of numerous publications, and a member of *Who's Who Worldwide*, *Who's Who in American Education*, and the *Who's Who Registry of Global Business Leaders*. He and his wife, Maryann, have a son, Michael, and a daughter, Katie.

DANIEL JAMES ROWLEY is currently a professor of management in the College of Business Administration at the University of Northern Colorado (UNC). From summer 1992 until fall 1995, he took a leave of absence from teaching to join the president's office at UNC to oversee the development of a university-wide strategic planning process. He worked directly with UNC's board of trustees to develop and approve strategic management policy for the university. During this time, he also served the university as chief of staff in the president's office and as secretary to the board of trustees, and helped formulate strategic priorities to guide the development of UNC's budgets. These efforts at UNC, which took Rowley beyond his experience in business strategic planning, were designed to uniquely fit the needs and characteristics of public higher education and resulted in growing national recognition for strategic planning in higher education.

In 1995 Rowley resumed his teaching, writing, and consulting activities. He currently works with other universities, school districts, and nonprofit organizations in their strategic planning efforts. He is cofounder and past president of the Institute of Behavioral and Applied Management, a national academic and professional organization for management professors, students, and practitioners. He is sole or lead author of a number of journal articles on the subjects of business management and strategic planning, and has given several national presentations on the same subjects. With UNC's current strategic planner, Donna Bottenberg, he has coauthored a chapter on strategic enrollment management published in 1996 in a scholarly casebook for the American Association of Collegiate Registrars and Admissions Officers.

Rowley received a B.A. degree (1969) in political science from the University of Colorado at Boulder. He earned an M.P.A. (Master of Public Administration) degree (1979) at the University of

Denver, and a Ph.D. degree (1987) in organizational management and strategic management at the University of Colorado at Boulder. He and his wife, Barbara, are the proud parents of one daughter, Rebecca.

HERMAN D. LUJAN has been president of the University of Northern Colorado (UNC) since December 1991. During his tenure he has established UNC as a teaching university whose first priority is to serve Colorado with high-quality undergraduate programs while bringing new energy and direction to its role as one of twenty-nine Doctoral I universities in the United States. In 1992 he initiated a campuswide strategic planning process designed to identify and better focus campus resources to help the university build on its strengths and develop a stronger fit with the needs of Colorado and the Rocky Mountain Region. In addition, he has launched a series of programs to help increase and improve the diversity of UNC's faculty, staff, and student body.

Lujan's career in higher education began at the University of Kansas (KU), where he was a faculty member in political science and an administrator for thirteen years. He was the director of KU's Institute for Social and Environmental Studies from 1972 to 1979, and took a one-year leave from 1974 to 1975 to serve as director of the Division of State Planning and Research in the Kansas governor's office. Immediately prior to coming to UNC, Lujan spent thirteen years at the University of Washington as a faculty member and administrator. He served as vice president for minority affairs before becoming vice provost in 1988, a position he held until he came to UNC. Lujan has worked on more than thirty research grant projects and has published numerous scholarly articles and books. He serves on the board of directors of Bank One Greeley and is active in several other civic, educational, and charitable organizations both locally and nationwide, including the American Council on Education (ACE), the American Association of State Colleges and Universities (AASCU), and the National Association of State Universities and Land Grant Colleges (NASULGC).

Lujan is a native of Hawaii and holds an A.B. degree (1958) from St. Mary's College in California, an M.A. degree (1960) from the University of California at Berkeley, and a Ph.D. degree (1964) from the University of Idaho, all in political science. He and his wife Carla are the parents of three children, and grandparents of six.

Working Toward Strategic Change

Introduction
The Strategic Planning Process

In our book *Strategic Change in Colleges and Universities*, we developed a comprehensive method of conducting a strategic planning process in a college or university. In this workbook, we present the basic steps of the process, and provide a series of examples and worksheets that those who are involved in a strategic planning exercise can use to help develop a comprehensive plan.

The workbook is primarily designed around a central model, what we have called the *strategic planning engine*. This model identifies the important components that form the foundation of the planning process (Dolence and Norris, 1994). It contains ten steps that we will address throughout this workbook. These steps constitute the *what-must-be-done* portion of the overall strategic planning process.

In our book we also discussed the process of implementing the strategic planning engine. This process is represented by a second model, the *strategic planning implementation process*, which consists of several key phases. These phases constitute the *how-to-do-it* portion of the overall strategic planning process. In the discussion that follows, we will present these two models of the strategic planning process briefly, and then build on both of them throughout the workbook. Thorough explanations of the strategic planning engine and the strategic planning process model are found in our book (see especially Chapters Six and Seven, respectively).

The Strategic Planning Engine

The strategic planning engine, depicted in Figure I.1, is a ten-step cyclical model that helps complex organizations make strategic decisions at any level of the strategic planning process. It provides a theoretically simple method for building the strategic planning process itself. It works equally well at the institutional, college, school, or departmental level, while also providing a consistent framework that ties each of these levels together automatically. At the same time, it is effective in keeping diverse groups of decision makers focused on the most important elements of the organization's success.

The ten steps of the strategic planning engine model are as follows:

1. Develop key performance indicators (KPIs).
2. Perform an external environmental assessment.
3. Perform an internal environmental assessment.
4. Perform a *s*trengths, *w*eaknesses, *o*pportunities, and *t*hreats (SWOT) analysis.
5. Conduct brainstorming.
6. Evaluate the potential impact of each idea on each strength, weakness, opportunity, and threat (cross-impact analysis).
7. Formulate strategies, mission, goals, and objectives.
8. Conduct a cross-impact analysis to determine the impact of the proposed strategies, goals, and objectives on the organization's ability to achieve its KPIs.
9. Finalize and implement strategies, goals, and objectives.
10. Monitor and evaluate actual impact of strategies, goals, and objectives on organizational KPIs.

In its graphic form (Figure I.1), the strategic planning engine appears linear, running from left to right and from Steps 1 through 10. In practice, however, those involved in college or university strategic planning can use the strategic planning engine to integrate many elements and practices that the organization has already identified or implemented. Many colleges and universities already have a set of management objectives that they can easily plug into the engine's evaluation chart. For example, a Total Quality Management (TQM) undertaking or the annual budget process will most likely have already identified and defined a set of KPIs that are crucial to the overall efficiency, operation, and effectiveness of the institution. Other ideas that could easily be translated into KPIs may have been included in requests in the annual budget process or in program change proposals. It is also likely that a college or university will have conducted a partial environmental analysis during an accreditation self-study or possibly as part of a fundraising market analysis. All of these components of organizational life can be plugged into the model; there is no need to reinvent them if they already exist.

The Strategic Planning Process Model

The strategic planning engine is a model of the various steps that should be taken in order to develop an effective strategic plan. *Performing* the steps is the concern of the second model we present here, which we explain in great detail in our book. The strategic planning process model helps organize the process and provides a series of phases that allow college and university strategic planning officers and strategic planning committees of both colleges and universities a logical method of developing the strategic planning engine. The following list outlines the stages of this process model; we then briefly explain each of the various stages and note where they occur in the steps of the strategic planning engine.

1. Select the initial planning committee.
2. Introduce the process.
3. Establish appropriate KPIs and organize key performance areas.
4. Survey the environment.
   a. Assess external opportunities and threats.
   b. Assess internal strengths and weaknesses.
   c. Perform a cross-impact analysis.
5. Share results with larger audience.
6. Develop definition and measurement criteria.
7. Measure current performance.
8. Establish five- and ten-year goals.
9. Determine strategies (using SWOT) in each KPI area.
10. Establish broad-based support.
    a. Develop appropriate policies for each KPI area.
    b. Begin the implementation process.
    c. Measure performance frequently.
    d. Perform one-year substantive review and modification.

Phase 1: Select the Initial Planning Committee

The first phase of the strategic planning process model involves the identification and selection of the members of the initial strategic

Figure I.1.

The Strategic Planning Engine.

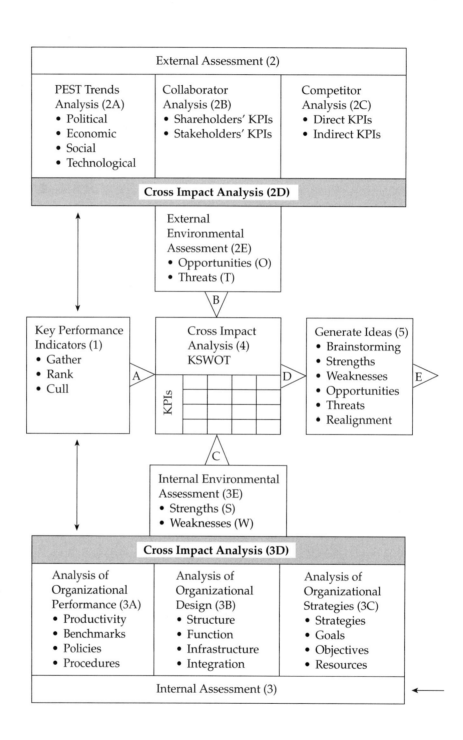

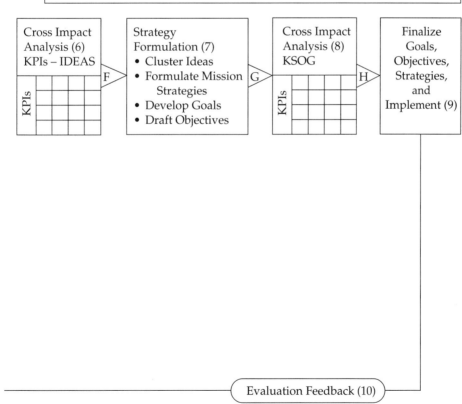

Strategic Planning Engine Deliverables Legend

A> List of Organizational Key Performance Indicators

B> Results of PEST, Collaborator, Competitor Analysis, List of Opportunities and Threats

C> Results of Internal Assessments, List of Organizational Strengths and Weaknesses

D> Document Detailing Impact of Internal and External Forces on Organizational Performance

E> List of Ideas on Permanent Record for Tracking and Referral

F> Formal Planning Team's Judgment on the Impact Each Idea Would Have on KPIs

G> A Mission and an Array of Targeted Strategies Aimed at Improving Organizational KPIs

H> Strategic Decisions That Accomplish Organizational Goals, Objectives, and Strategies

Cross Impact Analysis (6) KPIs – IDEAS	Strategy Formulation (7) • Cluster Ideas • Formulate Mission Strategies • Develop Goals • Draft Objectives	Cross Impact Analysis (8) KSOG	Finalize Goals, Objectives, Strategies, and Implement (9)

Evaluation Feedback (10)

planning committee (SPC). The first major decisions that the college or university needs to make are to identify the individual who will oversee the process—the strategic planner—and to consider who should be the members of the committee. The person selected to oversee the process must be responsible for organizing and for making operational decisions about how the process should unfold. As we argue in our book, this person should not be the president or chancellor but rather a respected faculty member who has broad campus support.

The SPC should include people who are dedicated to the well-being of the institution and who also reflect the broad constituency base of the campus. This broadness is needed to assure that the major elements of the institution or unit are adequately represented while at the same time the size of the group is kept manageable. With these people identified, it is appropriate that the president or chancellor give a charge to the group. It is very important to keep committee charges clean, concise, defined, and in context.

Phase 2: Introduce the Process

Introducing the process to the SPC and to the institution or unit is the second phase in the strategic planning process model. Here, outside assistance can be very valuable in providing substantive training for the planning group, and in providing information to the general campus through activities such as open forums. If the institution has decided not to use an outside person, someone internal needs to take responsibility for understanding the process (by becoming thoroughly familiar with the material in our book) and for training all the members of the SPC.

Phase 3: Establish Appropriate KPIs and Organize Key Performance Areas

This phase encompasses the establishment of KPIs. In developing the basis for planning, it is important to answer the questions, What are the most important outcomes of our performance in this institution/unit? And What are the most critical health factors of which we should be aware? These questions provide the framework for establishing campuswide or unitwide KPIs. As shown in Figure I.1, this is the first major step in the strategic planning engine.

Phase 4: Survey the Environment

In the fourth phase, the SPC surveys the institution's or unit's external and internal environments—steps two and three of the strategic planning engine. The strategic planner and the SPC need to manage the time required to perform these activities, particularly if the planning group already has a sense of which external and internal environmental forces are shaping the activities of the college or university. But beyond that, the process of inventorying these external and internal forces, calculating their effects on the direction of the institution, and identifying cause and effect relationships is a very useful exercise for the institution or unit because it yields a better sense of how the strategic planning process works. The SPC needs to refine the initial findings, in order both to identify and validate data and to prioritize results in order to establish which environmental elements are most critical to the health and well-being of the institution or unit. Based on these refined lists, the planning group can identify the organization's internal strengths and weaknesses and its external opportunities and threats.

Phase 5: Share Results with Larger Audience

This step consists of sharing the initial survey results with the larger campus, to help assure broad communication and engender support. The external and internal analyses conducted in Phase 4 often provide important new information regarding where the campus currently is and what is going on around it that dramatically affects it. This is important information for the entire campus (or unit) to better understand. Since these findings will form most of the base of the plan, communicating them to allow for a dialogue with campus interest groups is an important part of building a broader understanding of what planning yields.

Phases 6, 7, and 8: Definitions, Measurement Criteria, and Goals

The next three phases encompass the initial stages that create a strategic planning document. They also help those involved in the planning to think strategically about the institution and its environment. KPIs ultimately must be measurable, means of monitoring performance over time must be identified, and the direction the college or university hopes to follow must be articulated.

These phases occur after Step 4 of the strategic planning engine has led to a prioritized list of KPIs and a sense of how they interact with the various strengths, weakness, opportunities, and threats that the college or university has identified through the SWOT analysis as the most important factors of its environment. The SPC will begin implementing these concepts by taking the entire list of KPIs and dividing them into relevant activity areas to establish areas of concentration and analysis by subgroups that may form around them. While these areas of concentration provide some definition, each KPI must still be individually defined. The definition should include an explanation of what the KPI represents and how the group intends to measure it. KPIs related to quality present special problems. But even in these cases, broadly accepted surrogates can be used to provide approximate but acceptable measuring devices. For example, counting the number of articles published in top journals might serve as one surrogate for measuring faculty quality (though one measure alone is obviously not sufficient to provide an overall measure of many quality items).

Base-year performance measures are important because they provide the benchmarks from which planning will proceed. Some measures, such as enrollment, may be easy to do. Measures such as faculty productivity, however, may require new or surrogate measures. Regardless, all KPIs must be identified with a current measure, and from these, five- and ten-year goals can be established. As the plan is implemented, current measures tell how much progress the institution has made in achieving its identified goals.

The time required for appropriate goal setting is another very manageable activity. If large amounts of time are available, the planning group may wish to ask campus groups that work specifically in the areas affected to conduct feasibility studies and recommend specific five- and ten-year goals. If time and resources are scarce, it is not necessary for a group to conduct interviews and develop a best-guess set of goals. As a function of the one-year minimum requirement, such goals can be used initially, as estimates, and then revised at the end of the first year's activities. As the factors that affect best guesses are identified, a basis for revising five- and ten-year goals will emerge and the resulting set will be more accurate. While measurements should continue throughout the year, making the changes at the end of the year will allow decisions to be informed by ongoing analysis.

Phase 9: Determine Strategies (Using SWOT) in Each KPI Area

After the initial goals are set, the planning group is ready to engage in Phase 9, which coincide with Steps 7 and 8 of the strategic planning engine. First, long-term strategies are developed, which lead to identifying short-term strategies that the group believes will affect the institution's or unit's performance toward its desired goals. If the analyses of the college's, university's, or unit's internal and external environments are substantive and realistic, the group will be able to identify several viable strategies. They can do this by matching the strengths of the institution or unit to the opportunities found in the external environment, especially in those areas that are consistent with the goals set forward in the plan. At this point, all of the elements needed to construct the planning document are in place, and the group can proceed to the writing of a short, approximately fifteen-to-twenty-page encapsulation of the plan for broad internal and external distribution.

Phase 10: Establish Broad-Based Support

In Phase 10, implementation begins as prescribed in Step 9 of the strategic planning engine. It is now time for the SPC to provide the campus community or unit with the cumulative results and present status of the planning process. Distribution of the planning document, forums on and off campus, and other communication activities should be conducted to allow knowledge sharing, additional contributions, and advice from across the institution's or unit's community. To help underscore that strategic planning is a process and not an event, the document should be marked "draft" or "preliminary" and identified as a dated piece. The SPC should help the general community understand that the plan is emerging and that the opportunity remains open to contribute as the plan evolves. While some may see this openness as a flaw in the strategic planning process, *to be strategic and adaptive to change, the plan must remain flexible.* Since it is impossible to accurately predict the future, the plan must be allowed to adapt as new information becomes known. Having plans that are updated yearly or more frequently helps establish this central tenet of strategic planning as a dynamic process.

Considerations for Conducting the Process

The authors have used a variety of methods in conducting strategic planning exercises on college and university campuses. However, we have found three methods that we believe work most effectively: the use of decision support centers, spreadsheet templates, and paper forms. All of these approaches use brainstorming-types of decision-making processes. This section of the workbook will outline the key components of how an SPC might use each of these methods in developing its institutional strategic plan. The choice of which method to use will depend on availability and cost, and on the technology tolerance and general preferences of the group.

Tool 1: Brainstorming

Whether or not the committee uses outside consultants or other sources to coordinate and gather information, ultimately each group must identify, compile, organize, prioritize, and develop a working list of ideas that it will then use in the many steps we outline in the strategic planning process. We recommend that each group adopt *brainstorming* as their central method for conducting these idea-manipulation activities. We make this recommendation because it is important for each group to gather as much relevant information as possible, and to be sensitive to normal group decision-making dynamics: groups often tend to be dominated by one or two individuals, quieter people tend not to contribute, individual attitudes can often infect other members and influence their contributions, and people are often afraid to express an opinion because they fear that others will ridicule it.

Brainstorming is a method of group decision making designed to help overcome several of the tendencies just listed, and to produce results that are more complete and less parochial and that help establish group synergy. This method is governed by several rules that help make it more effective:

1. Participants must judge the ideas or contributions of others. Each item should be placed on a growing list without comment.

2. It is a good idea to allow participants to know what the exercise will entail prior to the session, and to encourage them to make personal lists ahead of time.

3. All items mentioned or listed should become part of the overall list, regardless of their seeming worth or usefulness; prioritization in later phases of the process will fix problems.

4. Each participant must agree to develop and contribute her or his ideas, concepts, or suggestions on the topic. Making suggestions for a list in a round-robin fashion often helps to assure that everyone has the opportunity to contribute.

5. Any participant may make additional suggestions to be added to a list, even though the group may have moved on to another task.

6. Once the list is complete, discussion of the list may commence, but reference to individuals who placed items on the list should be avoided, and questions about particular items should be asked of the group, not of an individual.

7. Keep the discussion as objective as possible, avoiding subjective and personal comments.

With these rules in mind, the group should become comfortable with the making of lists and the activities required to refine them to a point where the group feels it has a working list (a list they will use as they proceed through the next several steps of the process).

Tool 2: Decision Support Centers

One of the better computer-based technologies available for group decision-making is that of the decision support center. Unfortunately, these facilities are costly, and not every college or university has one. For those that do, however, and for those that can use one located nearby (usually at a cost to the group), decision support centers provide an extremely efficient and effective method of developing and prioritizing the several lists described throughout this workbook. They allow the group to brainstorm initial ideas, put them in categories, prioritize them, and make decisions about which of the ideas should survive as the ones the group will use to create its strategic plan.

A clear advantage of decision support centers is that each person works anonymously in adding ideas to the list, organizing them, prioritizing them, and coming up with a working list. Later, in the cross-impact analysis (during Step 2 of the strategic planning engine), the matrix analysis tool is excellent for quickly conducting the analysis of the data and interpreting the results. Normally a trained facilitator is required to use this technology and move the group through the dynamics of each exercise. The results, however, come quickly because of the technology, and the group can move through the exercises at a good speed with the use of such a facility.

One note of caution about the use of decision support facilities: it is important to monitor the energy level of the group as they work in these centers. Because these centers help people to work more quickly and efficiently, people will do a lot more in a shorter span of time—which is a benefit. However, the preparation and analysis of lists is hard work, particularly mentally. Some people organize their thoughts and act on them much more quickly than others, and these different rates of progress can come into conflict. For example, in prioritizing a list of fifty items, one person might be done in three minutes while another person will be done in thirty. The first person must sit quietly for twenty-seven minutes, or perhaps leave the room, but cannot go on to the next activity until everyone else is finished with this part of the program. The second person may begin to feel stress upon realizing that he or she is the only person still working. These situations add an extra dimension of fatigue to the group, which is also feeling the pressure of producing a large amount of work, and the group facilitator must know when the group has reached the level where further exercises would not be productive (and would possibly even be destructive). In such cases, more rather than fewer sessions in the center are most likely indicated, which will benefit the process but may strain the resources of the group. Nonetheless, the outcomes from all of the decision support center sessions that the authors have been a part of have proved that use of such facilities is the easiest and fastest way of gathering and sorting all the data created in an effective strategic planning exercise.

Tool 3: Spreadsheet Templates

A second method that requires the use of a computer but is more time-consuming than the decision support lab is the use of spreadsheet templates. The several forms we describe throughout this manual can be replicated on spreadsheets for use in Lotus 1–2–3, Excel, Quattro Pro, or another popular business spreadsheet program. The disadvantage of spreadsheets compared to the decision support centers is that only one person can input ideas from the group, and thus the anonymity aspect of the decision center setting is lost. The advantage of spreadsheets over the paper forms method, however, is that the spreadsheet can be easily organized, items can be easily shifted around, printouts of refined lists can serve as voting sheets, and votes can be tabulated to help establish priorities. When used in conjunction with a computer screen projection plate and a high-intensity overhead projector, participants can watch as the data comes together and is manipulated by the session facilitator. Users of the spreadsheet who like to see specific statistical inferences of the analyses can easily add "@" statements to calculate whatever statistical measure they might want to see.

Though a set of spreadsheet templates does not accompany this workbook, 3½-inch disks are available from the authors at a nominal charge (see the order form at the end of the workbook). Another option is to have someone create the spreadsheets, based on the forms found throughout the workbook, and then use them at a group decision-making session. Using spreadsheets also allows the forms found throughout this workbook to be used by individuals as tools for developing and bringing in personal ideas for each of the list types discussed in Steps One through Ten.

Tool 4: Paper Forms

This workbook contains a series of paper forms that groups can use to help themselves organize their activities as they conduct their strategic planning processes. These are forms we have created and used with college and university planning groups to develop the data criteria that have formed the foundation on which they have developed their strategic plans. They are for both individual and group uses (as noted on each form), and can help provide specific tools to allow individuals and groups to gather, organize, analyze, and develop working data lists. Because the information provided on these forms is typically handwritten by participants and then by groups as they collect the data, this is the most time-consuming method of developing the database for a strategic plan. Also, the group must separate lists, develop voting sheets, and calculate results—activities that take additional time.

We do not mean to suggest that the use of paper forms is not a good method. On the contrary, this method does encourage participation and creative thinking, just as the other methods do, and the forms we present in this workbook provide a method that assures that the group will cover all the essential bases to assure that it has adequate data with which to develop its strategic plan. Used within the general rules of brainstorming, this is a very successful method of conducting the process. Where no decision support center exists and the group does not wish to use spreadsheet templates, the forms will be effective in guiding the group to a successful conclusion.

Use of paper forms might also add to the ease of the experience. For example, before coming to the session in which the group will work with KPIs, having each member of the group develop a list before the session on the forms provided in this workbook will help expedite all three methods by providing some initial ideas with which to work and that can be augmented by additional ideas that the group generates during the session.

Definitions

Before we go through the development of the steps involved in creating the elements of the strategic planning engine, a few definitions are in order:

Aligning: recognizing and exploiting knowledge about an institution's strengths, weaknesses, opportunities, and threats to achieve congruity between the institution and the environment, a dynamic equilibrium of the ecosphere of an institution and its environment.

Environment: the political, social, economic, technological, and educational ecosystem, both internal and external to the organization, within which the college or university resides.

Goals: the major milestones that have a two- to five-year, or even longer, horizon. An example might be reaching a retention rate of 75 percent in ten years, from a current retention rate of 60 percent.

Objectives: the outcomes of no more than one year; they tend to be time bound (assigned due dates) and measurable (their achievement can be unambiguously determined) activities that keep the organization or unit heading toward its goals. An example of an objective that would support the goal in the previous example might be to increase the retention rate to 62 percent during the upcoming academic year. (*Note:* for the purposes of the present discussion, we will adhere to these more precise definitions for the terms *goals* and *strategies*.)

Strategic: that which relates to the relationship between the institution and its environment.

Strategic decision making: making the optimal choice or the choice that best fits the needs of the institution's strategic plan or strategic management.

Strategic learning: the institutional process of learning from successes and failures for the purpose of informing the institution during the next stages of the strategic planning or strategic management process.

Strategic management: the assurance that the institution's attention and focus are applied to maintain an optimal alignment with the environment.

Strategic planning: a formal process designed to help an organization identify and maintain an optimal alignment with the most important elements of its environment.

Strategic thinking: arraying options through a process of opening up institutional thinking to a range of alternatives and decisions that identify the best fit between the institution, its resources, and the environment.

Strategy: an agreed-upon course of action and direction that changes the relationship or maintains an alignment that helps to assure a more optimal relationship between the institution and its environment.

Tactics: the operational methods that form the building blocks used to implement the strategy. For example, the strategy of focusing on community college transfers to increase enrollments might be partially achieved by using a tactic of offering specific scholarships to community college students with a grade point average of 3.0.

Finally, a word about the planning vocabulary. We use terms such as KPIs, SWOT analysis, PEST, and so forth. These are exemplary and not absolute terms. Each campus should use comfortable local terminology and be flexible about it. For example, KPIs can become "performance measures," and policies can become "priorities."

Developing Key Performance Indicators

Key performance indicators (KPIs) are required to measure the outcomes of the various phases and steps in the strategic planning process. As measures, KPIs should be specific, simple, and quantifiable. The development of KPIs will ensure that goals, values, objectives, and guiding concepts are practical. KPIs should be obvious and operational to any user or person reviewing the plan. This step takes strategic planners through the process of identifying appropriate KPIs, prioritizing them, and then devising a set of working KPIs to guide the process.

Gather, Rank, and Cull KPIs

The analytical side of the strategic planning engine is based on organizational KPIs. This fact is important because the KPIs anchor the decisions that are generated through the strategic planning engine. The strategic planning engine is designed to help all participating decision makers to explore and understand fully the relationships among the organization, the objectives the organization seeks to achieve, and the general environmental forces with which the organization must deal. As such, the strategic planning engine represents an effective method for helping the organization to remain aligned with its environment. Such alignment is guided by the results of a cross-impact analysis (Tool 5, which we discuss in Step 2), a modified Delphi decision-making technique that gives the strategic planning committee (SPC) a clear vision of how a particular set of factors affects the achievement of the organization's KPIs. It does this by illuminating the impact of external and internal environmental strengths, weaknesses, opportunities, and threats (SWOT) on the organization's ability to achieve its KPIs.

Procedurally, an important question is, How many KPIs should a campus or unit identify? The answer is that the appropriate number of KPIs is situational. Having too many KPIs leads to a cumbersome and complicated process that normally will lead to frustration and early disenchantment with strategic planning. This is because the scope of activities needed to build a plan with many KPIs will be far greater than anyone has time or patience to attempt. Conversely, having too few KPIs means there are not enough performance touch points to develop and monitor a cohesive strategy. In our experience, an initial set of twelve to twenty university-wide KPIs appears to be a reasonable number, providing that the group believes the items included encompass an adequate range of important organizational outcomes and related measures.

When participants understand the context of the plan and their role in its implementation, many of the emerging ideas can be implemented immediately. Individuals and units can begin to align their behavior and focus on the needs generated by the strategic planning engine. Practitioners report that payback is often immediate and that at each step new insights generate new enthusiasm.

It is important at the outset of the planning process for the planning committee to develop an understanding of the core elements that determine the success or failure of the college or university. Unlike mission-driven planning, building a strategic planning process on the base of such an understanding ties the institution directly into those areas that are most crucial to its ongoing development and long-term survival.

The Central Role of KPIs

The realignment of higher education with its environments means that colleges and universities must recognize their roles and responsibilities in relation to a variety of internal and external constituencies. There really is no effective way of doing this other than to check performance against expectations (both the expectations that institutions have developed for themselves and the expectations of their constituents). Unlike mission-driven planning, planning that is based on a premise of measuring and checking performance against expectations provides an important and highly beneficial linkage between the institution and its environment. KPIs are the linchpins that tie the most essential operations of the college or university to the strategic planning process.

For the purposes of this discussion, we shall define a KPI in the following manner:

> A key performance indicator is a measure of an essential outcome of a particular organizational performance activity, or an important indicator of a precise health condition of an organization.

A couple of examples of performance-outcome KPIs might include academic year-end undergraduate full-time equivalent (FTE) enrollment, and academic year-end graduate degrees granted. Some examples of health-condition KPIs might include total state allocations from year to year, the presence or absence of public law that reflects institutional expectations, the overall reputation of the college or university, and the percentage of scheduled maintenance performed on the campus during a given year.

The foundation of the strategic planning engine is a family of organizational KPIs. KPIs are reasonably precise values that have one and only one definition throughout the organization. Normally, a college or university SPC will gather KPIs in a brainstorming session, especially as the process becomes more formalized. The primary question for this brainstorming session is, What are the measures that our stakeholders and managers use to determine whether we are successful? The strength of the KPIs is not so much in individual measures but in taking the organizational KPIs as a family of measures that compete and collaborate with each other.

KPIs as Performance Indicators

As the definition provided earlier indicates, there are two types of measures that constitute key performance indicators. The first has to do with the measurement of a specific outcome of an essential activity of the organization over which the institution has control. Essential activities are those that have direct bearing on the perceived well-being and success of the institution. Some of these activities may well be critical to the survival of the institution.

In preparation for determining what constitutes a list of most essential performance activities and the outcomes they generate, the institution needs to develop a profile of itself that details which of its activities are most essential to its survival and success. The subject matter of this research and discussion will include the financial performance of the college or university, the effectiveness of its academic program base, its academic reputation, its administrative operations, its patterns of communication, and its ability to fulfill the expectations of significant internal and external constituencies. The college's or university's SPC should initiate this process and analyze its results.

As brainstorming sessions begin it is important to ensure that the data are as objective as possible. Unfortunately, many of the opinions that committee members give to develop the list of activities and outcomes may not be objective. It is important, therefore, for the committee members who are accumulating this data to attempt to verify that the items that appear to receive strong support are identified and measured as accurately as possible. Further, while some KPIs are straightforward, such as meeting and balancing budgets, others are much more difficult to determine, such as the quality of the faculty.

Measurement is a substantial part of this process and it is important for planners to recognize that certain potential KPIs, such as program quality, will raise potentially serious political issues. Nonetheless, it is important to develop a list of overall performance areas from which the most important KPIs can be culled, regardless of the political constraints of the campus.

KPIs as Health Conditions

The second part of the definition of a KPI has to do with the measurement of a condition that affects the health and well-being of the institution, a condition over which the institution may have little or no control, or a considerable amount of control. It may or may not be particularly useful to set goals for these conditions or devise strategies that the institution hopes will substantially alter them. For instance, the final determination of what a state allocates to a college or university is not something for which an institution ordinarily sets goals, yet it is critical for the campus to know what these figures are, and what the trends are that lead to their establishment or from which they emanate. Using this information the SPC can forecast anticipated allocations, based on past and current trends, and reasonably determine appropriate KPIs that will measure actual outcomes over time. Likewise, the public's opinion of a college or university is crucial, but it is usually resistant to public relations activities designed to affect it one way or another. Conversely, if an institution wishes to be considered one of the top ten in the country in a particular category, this performance indicator is measurable.

These examples of external forces with which an institution must deal reflect critical environmental elements that an institution must consider but which they may not control. A reality that many public institutions face is that legal prohibitions exist that prevent or limit them from even attempting to try to influence outside constituencies. Nonetheless, since these types of external constituencies can have a significant effect on the operation of an institution, it is important to identify these conditions and then designate them as KPIs in order to monitor their impact on the institution.

Establishing Priorities

The activities involved in developing a comprehensive list of KPIs will result in a set of KPIs that on the surface may not be particularly useful. Some of the KPIs on the list will be quite important, while others will be less clear or not as important.

To develop an effective working set of KPIs, the SPC needs to develop a scheme for prioritizing. As the planning process identifies overall performance factors and health factors, it is also important to develop a common understanding about which of the factors are most vital, and which will have longer-term effects than others.

It is not unusual for initial lists to include performance areas and health factors that do not have long-term strategic implications. For example, a disruption of a college's activities due to the sudden departure of a dean is not a long-term strategic issue and should not be on any list of KPIs to be monitored over time. However, a long-standing history of strong differences between faculty and administration *is* a strategic issue. Such an item should most likely be on the list, even though the SPC may not initially feel that it is a top priority. The ability to understand the difference between these two concerns is related to the issues of strategic thinking and strategic decision making. As the SPC becomes more familiar and comfortable with thinking strategically, the quality of the KPIs will improve and the process will move forward more easily.

In developing a final list of KPIs, the aim is to create a list that is short enough to handle within the planning process yet important enough to be representative of the long-term growth and survival of the institution. Since most committee members will be newcomers to this approach to planning, getting a final list can be difficult. Yet keeping focused on such a list within well-understood time lines is one of the more important activities of the SPC.

Levels of KPIs

As KPIs emerge from the process, some will reflect the highest level of the organization and others will reflect secondary levels, as shown in Figure 1.1. For example, annual institutional FTE enrollment numbers reflect the aggregated enrollments of the institution at the overall level. Yet within these numbers there are most likely

Figure 1.1.
Levels of KPIs.

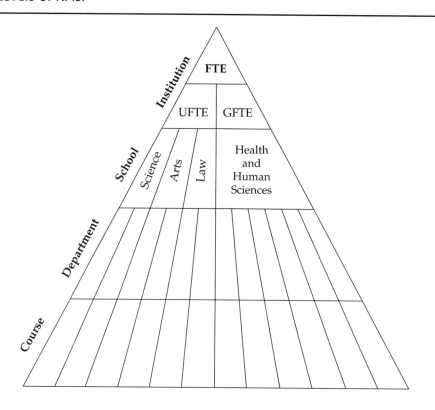

several composite enrollment figures, including term, college, school, department, and course enrollments. To go further with this example, while the university's business school might have an enrollment KPI that contributes to the institution's overall KPI, within the business school, the departments of accounting, finance, and marketing and the MBA program should also have enrollment KPIs that contribute to the school's KPI. KPIs thus form a pyramid, with the organization-wide KPIs sitting at the top, the division KPIs sitting one layer underneath, and major unit and department level KPIs forming the foundation. Annual institutional FTE enrollment represents a primary KPI while the FTE enrollments of units and departments are considered secondary KPIs. Secondary should not imply and does not mean less important. To the contrary, one can see that without the component enrollments there would be no annual institutional FTE enrollment.

Characteristics of KPIs

As members of the SPC develop the initial list of KPIs, they need to focus on several specific KPI characteristics:

1. *Measurement:* Are the measures currently available or must they be collected?

2. *Value:* If the measure is currently available, what is the current value? It is probably important to avoid a discussion of what the measurements should be or of whether the KPI is worth collecting until after the internal and external environmental assessments are conducted.

3. *Level:* Is each KPI primary (highest level) or secondary (a contributing factor to a primary) in scope?

4. *Definition:* Precisely how is each KPI defined? The unambiguous definition of each KPI is extremely important and should be developed during the compilation process.

Definitions and Measurement Criteria

We have suggested that those involved in the initial phases of strategic planning should establish the proper base before going further. Once this base is in place, the next steps can be taken. One of the first steps in establishing the base is to give an operational definition to each KPI and develop a related scheme of measurement. Also, it is important to recognize and use the prevailing campus data dictionary to develop the KPIs. For example, in the case of program quality, KPIs may be associated with a significant parochial and political element, and it will be important for the definitions and measures to be as widely acceptable to the campus community as possible.

Getting different groups involved in developing definitions and measures is an appropriate way of establishing greater campus buy-in and furthering participation. Though it may take more time to involve such groups than not to involve them, soliciting comment on potentially controversial items from the groups that are the most affected by them will pay off down the road with fewer arguments, and will eliminate the conjecture that important segments of the community were not involved with the development of the plan. It is evident that in establishing a definition and measure for something as potentially controversial as, for example, faculty quality, representative bodies of the faculty should be consulted. If particular campus bodies fail to respond in a timely or constructive manner, it may be acceptable (though not particularly wise) to move forward without them—but it is important in any event to have asked for comment. Our experience has proven that those who are particularly intent on stopping or hindering the strategic planning process use lack of inclusion above all other reasons as their major criticism.

In this initial part of the construction of the planning foundation it is important that the planners take care to encourage patience. Often participants do not want to wade through the complexity of a definition, preferring to delegate the task to a subgroup. Yet experience suggests that delegation should only be done after consensus on basic parameters is reached. Exhibit 1.1

Exhibit 1.1.

Examples of KPIs with Definitions.

KPI	Definition
1. Undergraduate FTE Enrollment	Number of total units attempted divided by 15
2. Graduate FTE Enrollment	Number of total units attempted divided by 12
3. Tuition Revenue	Tuition revenue collected net of institutional financial aid
4. Graduation Rate	Percentage of full-time undergraduates who graduate in four years
5. Minority Enrollment	Percentage of all enrolled students who are minorities
6. Placement Rate	Percentage of graduates employed or in advanced study one year after graduation
7. Student-Faculty Ratio	Number of FTE students divided by number of FTE faculty
8. Recruitment Yield	Percentage of students offered admission who enroll
9. Retention Rate	Percentage of students who maintain satisfactory progress
10. Break-Even Major Index	Total revenue deriving from students in each major minus the attributable cost of the major department
11. Average Debt Burden	Total value of loans divided by the number of loan recipients
12. Student Satisfaction	Composite score from annual student needs and priorities survey
13. Average SAT Score	Average SAT score of incoming freshmen
14. Value of Endowment	Book value of endowment at the end of each quarter
15. Deferred Maintenance	Dollar value of maintenance backlog

provides fifteen examples of KPIs with definitions derived from actual planning processes.

Eventually, when the planning process links strategic decisions with KPIs, the result can be especially effective in aligning a college or university with its environment, prioritizing resource allocations and program initiatives, focusing attention, and setting a course of action for the organization as a whole. KPIs allow concrete specification of the milestones and indicators that mark institutional progress. In short, they guide the organization, ensuring that it becomes more effective and more competitive.

How to Operationalize KPIs

Once the SPC has identified a suitable set of KPIs, adequately defined them, and appropriately categorized the list, it is time to calculate the measures of these KPIs for the most recent available time period. This is also a good time to add trend data, providing that it is available. As they formulate this basic data set, planners should also construct a KPI update calendar to articulate each data cycle and identify when new numbers will be available, who will collect them, and who will be responsible for the calculations, reports, and distribution that result.

From this point forward, the KPIs form the foundation of the strategic planning process. It is important, therefore, for everyone involved to use the same set of numbers. Any issues of multiple sources must also be resolved at this point.

KPIs provide a means for measuring each of the major elements in an institution's strategic plan. The measures summarize whether or not an expected outcome or goal has been achieved. In addition, if an outcome is not achieved, the KPI provides a basis for identifying what was not accomplished and what should be changed. Well-developed KPIs can also indicate the direction in which behavior must be adjusted to obtain the desired outcome.

For example, one university KPI might be minority enrollment. This is an important KPI because of the mission of the institution, the changing demographics of the service area, and the general need for the institution to be more diverse in its student, faculty, and staff makeup and its program. Minorities are a major source of enrollment growth. A KPI might be worded as "minorities as a percentage of undergraduate enrollment." The working definition of a person classified as a minority might be "anyone of a protected class under Federal rules and law, or similarly identified under state law." Measurement would be straightforward. For example, after reviewing the census of the institution, the present

Exhibit 1.2.

Possible College or University KPIs, Definitions, Measures, and Goals.

FTE Graduate Enrollment: The measure of full-time-equivalent graduate student enrollments on an annualized basis (including summer, fall, and spring enrollments) as calculated yearly by the Office of Institutional Research.

Current Level (1994–1995)	3,544
Base-Year Level (1992–1993)	3,308
Five-Year Goal (1997–1998)	3,700
Ten-Year Goal (2002–2003)	4,000

Alumni Attitude Audit: The percentage of alumni who rated their satisfaction with the general undergraduate or graduate experience as very good or excellent, as reported annually by the university's alumni office as a result of a random sampling of 1,000 alumni who graduated within the last ten years.

Current Level (1995)	76 percent
Base-Year Level (1993)	75 percent
Five-Year Goal (1998)	77.5 percent
Ten-Year Goal (2003)	80 percent

percentage of minorities is determined to be 12 percent. A similar review of enrollments in high schools and community colleges indicates a percentage of 25 percent. This number can become the goal for the institution to achieve (to better mirror its service area) over a reasonable number of years, as shown in Exhibit 1.2.

The working set of KPIs that results from this exercise should be divided into classes of KPIs, such as enrollment management, academic, resources, or other areas that lend themselves to strategic planning. The number should be small at this point—no more than twenty. This number may grow over time, but at the outset, a smaller number allows the group to focus better and develop straightforward strategies.

Hints

1. Spend time to make sure that participants know what a KPI is, and that they agree on the working list. Also be sure that participants agree on the values of the specific measures for each KPI. Again, *take your time* here. KPIs are the foundation of the strategic plan, and your group will suffer later on if it has not selected KPIs that are workable and acceptable to everyone.

2.   In the example of minority enrollment as a KPI provided in the previous section (a KPI that may well appear on most college and university campuses), planners would be wise to survey schools and community colleges who historically have had good success in minority enrollments.

3.   Keep the number of KPIs small at first. There will be a tendency to write many. The authors have been in situations in which the planning group has come up with in excess of a hundred KPIs, all of which the group felt were important. This is an unwieldy number, and would create many problems. Be sure to ask, Is this item essential to effectively measuring the performance of the institution? Remember that what is needed is an effective rather than an exhaustive set of KPIs.

Worksheets

The following pages contain worksheets that both individuals and groups can use to develop their initial list of KPIs, to organize them, to prioritize them, to develop a working list, and finally, to put definitions to the final list. The lists that the authors have designed to be completed by individuals contain the word *individual* in the upper right-hand corner, and the lists that are to be completed by groups contain the word *group* in the upper right-hand corner.

Go through the forms in order. Regardless of the method your group is using (decision support center, spreadsheet, or paper forms), all participants should fill out the first form in this section (Worksheet 1.1) to be better prepared for the first group session. After completing that form, groups using the decision support center method should use the forms as a guide for the decisions the group will make as they move through the exercises. Groups using spreadsheets will find these forms duplicated on the disk available from the authors, or they can create their own based on the forms found here.

After completing Worksheet 1.1, the group should collect data from all participants following the instructions on Worksheet 1.2. When all the data is collected, it must be organized and prioritized. Worksheet 1.3 provides instructions for completing this step. Worksheet 1.4 is a list of the surviving KPIs—a working list that results from the activities of prioritizing. Finally, Worksheet 1.5 provides a format for adding definitions and current measurements to each of the KPIs.

On the disk that is obtainable from the authors, the spreadsheet templates for this step can be found in the file "Step1."

WORKSHEET 1.1   Individual

Essential Outcomes of Performance

Prior to the session in which the strategic planning committee (SPC) will develop its list of key performance indicators (KPIs), write out at least three items in each of the following categories. These items will be either essential outcomes or important health measures for the appropriate category. For example, "knowledgeable students" might be an example of an essential outcome in the academic category, and "state appropriations" might be an example of an important health condition in the resources category.

Academic:

1.

2.

3.

Enrollments:

1.

2.

3.

Administrative:

1.

2.

3.

Resources (finances, budgets, personnel):

1.

2.

3.

Campus support programs and facilities:

1.

2.

3.

WORKSHEET 1.1   *continued*

Information technology:

    1.

    2.

    3.

Other:

    1.

    2.

    3.

Essential Outcomes of Performance

The strategic planning committee (SPC) will use this form (or a black/white board or a large pad of paper) to develop its initial list of key performance indicators (KPIs). The group facilitator will write down the ideas that individuals have generated by asking each person to contribute one item at a time. When all the items that people have previously identified have been added to the list, participants should add any additional items they have thought of since writing their own lists. Do not be constrained by the number of items on these lists; add numbers to accommodate all the ideas that individuals and the group generate.

Academic:

1.   7.
2.   8.
3.   9.
4.   10.
5.   11.
6.   12.

Enrollments:

1.   7.
2.   8.
3.   9.
4.   10.
5.   11.
6.   12.

Administrative:

1.   7.
2.   8.
3.   9.
4.   10.
5.   11.
6.   12.

WORKSHEET 1.2 *continued*

Resources (finances, budgets, personnel):

1.		7.	
2.		8.	
3.		9.	
4.		10.	
5.		11.	
6.		12.	

Campus support programs and facilities:

1.		7.	
2.		8.	
3.		9.	
4.		10.	
5.		11.	
6.		12.	

Information technology:

1.		7.	
2.		8.	
3.		9.	
4.		10.	
5.		11.	
6.		12.	

Other:

1.		7.	
2.		8.	
3.		9.	
4.		10.	
5.		11.	
6.		12.	

WORKSHEET 1.3   Group

Selecting the Master Set of KPIs

Once the group has established its full list of KPIs, it should eliminate duplicates, and any items that the group as a whole feels do not belong on the list (for such reasons as that the item is not related to the category, that it does not exist as a condition or issue affecting the campus, or that it truly is not important). Keep this discussion objective. Then use this form to list the items that survive and to make sure that each fits one of the planning categories.

Academic:

1.

2.

3.

4.

5.

6.

7.

8.

9.

Enrollments:

1.

2.

3.

4.

5.

6.

7.

8.

9.

WORKSHEET 1.3   *continued*

Administrative:

1.

2.

3.

4.

5.

6.

7.

8.

9.

Resources (finances, budgets, personnel):

1.

2.

3.

4.

5.

6.

7.

8.

9.

Campus support programs and facilities:

1.

2.

3.

4.

5.

6.

7.

8.

9.

WORKSHEET 1.3 *continued*

Information technology:

1.

2.

3.

4.

5.

6.

7.

8.

9.

Other:

1.

2.

3.

4.

5.

6.

7.

8.

9.

WORKSHEET 1.4   Group

Refining the Working List of KPIs

After the group has refined the reduced list of KPIs in each category, as directed on Worksheet 1.3, enter the top most important KPIs on this form. Include only the most important KPIs on this list. It is best if you have no more than two or three KPIs for each area, though space is provided for 4. Don't worry about the small number now. Over time, you can add more as experience identifies other KPIs that should be more closely controlled and monitored. At this point it is best to keep the number to those that are the most important.

Academic:

1.

2.

3.

4.

Enrollments:

1.

2.

3.

4.

Administrative:

1.

2.

3.

4.

Resources (finances, budgets, personnel):

1.

2.

3.

4.

Campus support programs and facilities:

    1.

    2.

    3.

    4.

Information technology:

    1.

    2.

    3.

    4.

Other:

    1.

    2.

    3.

    4.

KPIs, Definitions and Current Measures

The final part of the first step of the strategic planning engine is to develop definitions for each KPI and to determine its current measurement. Again, use brainstorming to help develop the definition and try to arrive at a consensus agreement. If this is not possible, it is permissible to vote on a broadly agreed-upon, clarifying, and informative definition. See previous examples for direction. Also, determine the current measure. Remember, qualitative measures may require a surrogate. If you use a surrogate, be sure it is part of your definition. List the results of your deliberations and investigations on this form to complete Step 1.

Academic:

KPI: _____   Defined as: _____

_____

_____

Current Measure: _____

KPI: _____   Defined as: _____

_____

_____

Current Measure: _____

KPI: _____   Defined as: _____

_____

_____

Current Measure: _____

KPI: _____   Defined as: _____

_____

_____

Current Measure: _____

WORKSHEET 1.5 *continued*

Enrollments:

KPI: _____   Defined as: _____
_____
_____

Current Measure: _____

KPI: _____   Defined as: _____
_____
_____

Current Measure: _____

KPI: _____   Defined as: _____
_____
_____

Current Measure: _____

KPI: _____   Defined as: _____
_____
_____

Current Measure: _____

Administrative:

KPI: _____   Defined as: _____
_____
_____

Current Measure: _____

KPI: _____   Defined as: _____
_____
_____

Current Measure: _____

WORKSHEET 1.5 *continued*

KPI: _____ Defined as: _____

_____

_____

Current Measure: _____

KPI: _____ Defined as: _____

_____

_____

Current Measure: _____

Resources (finances, budgets, personnel):

KPI: _____ Defined as: _____

_____

_____

Current Measure: _____

KPI: _____ Defined as: _____

_____

_____

Current Measure: _____

KPI: _____ Defined as: _____

_____

_____

Current Measure: _____

KPI: _____ Defined as: _____

_____

_____

Current Measure: _____

WORKSHEET 1.5   *continued*

Campus support programs and facilities:

KPI: _____   Defined as: _____

_____

_____

Current Measure: _____

KPI: _____   Defined as: _____

_____

_____

Current Measure: _____

KPI: _____   Defined as: _____

_____

_____

Current Measure: _____

KPI: _____   Defined as: _____

_____

_____

Current Measure: _____

WORKSHEET 1.5   *continued*

Information technology:

KPI: _____   Defined as: _____

_____

_____

Current Measure: _____

KPI: _____   Defined as: _____

_____

_____

Current Measure: _____

KPI: _____   Defined as: _____

_____

_____

Current Measure: _____

KPI: _____   Defined as: _____

_____

_____

Current Measure: _____

WORKSHEET 1.5 *continued*

Other:

KPI: _____   Defined as: _____

_____

_____

Current Measure: _____

KPI: _____   Defined as: _____

_____

_____

Current Measure: _____

KPI: _____   Defined as: _____

_____

_____

Current Measure: _____

KPI: _____   Defined as: _____

_____

_____

Current Measure: _____

STEP 2

Assessing the
External Environment

Planning does not take place in a vacuum. Every institution has a context of both internal and external forces within which it operates. Step 2 looks specifically at the effects of the external forces and the impact they have on the institution.

The SWOT Analysis

The institution's external forces include the local community, the business and professional communities, a rapidly changing economy, the surrounding demography, competitive institutions, the global marketplace, technology, communications, and an array of friends and alumni. By identifying the most salient of these forces, the strategic planners can begin to understand the relationship that exists between the college or university and its constituents. The SWOT analysis (analysis of strengths, weaknesses, opportunities, and threats) is perhaps the clearest and most straightforward manner of doing this. Exhibit 2.1 contains an example of the results of a SWOT analysis. (As the exhibit illustrates, the SWOT analysis is also used to identify internal environmental forces; analysis of the internal environment is discussed in the next chapter.)

The analysis of the external environment is more difficult than the analysis of the internal environment. There are obstacles to identifying the crucial stakeholders of an institution, and to understanding what they need from the institution and their claims upon it. However difficult this information is to obtain, it must be

Exhibit 2.1.

Examples of Campus SWOTs.

Possible Campus SWOTs

(Strengths, Weaknesses, Opportunities, and Threats)

Internal		External	
Strengths	Weaknesses	Opportunities	Threats
• increasing applications	• high dependence upon state support	• new international programs	• increasing state scrutiny
• new technology building	• generally deteriorating physical plant	• new governmental contracts	• reduced US support of grants and contracts
• nationally-known faculty	• too many full-professors	• new academic program areas	• growing competition among state schools

acquired as reasonably as possible. Although stakeholders are numerous and differ in their claims and expectations, an inventory of stakeholders is necessary and should include at least those that maintain normal contact with the university. These groups range from legislators, parents, lobbyists, grant coordinators, recruiters, marketing specialists, and professionals served by the university's degree programs to consultants, alumni, business leaders, governmental officials, influential community members, and the media. In addition, survey reports, assessment reports, accreditation studies, and other formal analyses can be found and can add significantly to the database for this evaluation.

The results of collecting and analyzing such data—a list of *opportunities* and a list of *threats*—should help the strategic planning committee (SPC) to understand the contexts and conditions of the institution's external stakeholder coalitions. These lists of opportunities and threats should also enable the strategic planners to compare the services the college or university currently provides with the services it should or might provide. With this knowledge, strategic planners can decide how best to match what the institution does with what the external stakeholders need or desire most. With this new level of understanding, planners will be in a better position to strengthen the foundation for substantive and effective planning by ascertaining the appropriate vision for the institution and its most essential areas of performance.

External Environmental Analysis

Once the SPC has identified the initial set of KPIs, it is ready to turn its attention to the external environment. The strategic plan-

Figure 2.1.
Strategic Planning Engine Step 2.

External Assessment (2)		
PEST Trends Analysis (2A) • Political • Economic • Social • Technological	Collaborator Analysis (2B) • Shareholders' KPIs • Stakeholders' KPIs	Competitor Analysis (2C) • Direct KPIs • Indirect KPIs
Cross Impact Analysis (2D)		
	External Environmental Assessment (2E) • Opportunities (O) • Threats (T)	

ning engine characterizes the external environment in terms of three domains: (1) PEST (political, economic, sociological, and technological) trends, (2) collaborators, and (3) competitors, including the student market. The external environmental analysis focuses group attention on identifying and analyzing the impact that external environmental factors within these three domains will have on each of the organization's KPIs (see Figure 2.1).

Use of the cross-impact analysis tool helps the institution's SPC to identify which of the domain forces have an important effect on the college or university. The SPC can then use the resulting information to evaluate the fit between the institution and the environments that have relevant claims on or ties to it. The strategic planning engine looks at these domains using a specific analytical method.

PEST Trends Analysis

The first set of external domain forces is defined by a PEST analysis, which evaluates *p*olitical, *e*conomic, *s*ociological, and *t*echnological trends and events. The purpose of the PEST analysis is threefold. First, it illuminates trends and events that may have a positive or negative impact on the organization's health. Second, it furnishes the SPC with an in-depth understanding of these factors and their effects. Third, and most important, the PEST analysis determines the degree to which the organization is properly aligned with the full range of significant factors in its environment. By focusing on changes in this particular environmental set, the analysis highlights where these changes can create misalignments unless the college or university takes anticipatory action.

The PEST analysis helps the SPC avoid three frequent pitfalls of the planning process. First, the analysis identifies weak environmental signals the presence of which may not be widely felt or understood by the organization but which may have significant impact. Unfortunately, most organizations usually avoid this category of environmental factors. Second, the PEST analysis also recognizes that the importance and impact of each trend and event is different. This understanding allows the group to focus attention on the more important external forces, and to minimize time and effort devoted to less influential ones. Finally, the PEST analysis avoids "paralysis by analysis" by focusing attention on only the trends and events that impact the KPIs.

By viewing these environmental forces through the lens of the KPIs (using cross-impact analysis), the PEST analysis is much more focused than traditional environmental scanning analyses. This focus comes from the process of centering discussion and analysis on the impact that specific environmental trends and events have on specific aspects of organizational performance.

Once the most important PEST trends and events are identified, their potential impact on the organizational KPIs is assessed. During the PEST analysis, the SPC is likely to discover that it has omitted an important KPI that should be monitored. That KPI can be added to the list after appropriate discussion and the analysis can be continued. In this way the analysis serves to inform the strategic planning process, and the process corrects itself for deficiencies as the SPC works through it.

Tool 5: Cross-Impact Analysis

Analyzing the data that the SWOT analysis has generated can be done through the use of a cross-impact analysis. The cross-impact analysis is a technique for harvesting the collective judgment of the group and for focusing group discussion and supporting analysis. It is a useful tool that helps identify the effects of particular events or issues on the key performance indicators the group developed in Step 1. It is conducted using a two-dimensional matrix, as shown in the example in Table 2.1, in which KPIs are arrayed down the rows, and the environmental factors—in the example, political, economic, sociological, and technological trends and events—are arrayed across the columns. Each SPC member involved in the analysis assesses the impact that he or she believes each trend and event could have on each KPI. The appropriate impact is marked using, in the case of the example, the following scale:

6 = strong positive influence

5 = moderate positive influence

4 = weak positive influence

3 = weak negative influence

2 = moderate negative influence

1 = strong negative influence

0 = neutral, don't know, no impact, not applicable

Please note that the scale used for the example is not the only option for scoring a cross-impact analysis. In fact, a number of alternatives can and have been used. The scale must accommodate a range of judgments regarding the impact of the PEST trend or event on a particular KPI. When conducted by an individual using the sample scale, a cross-impact analysis might look like the example presented in Table 2.2.

Analysis of Collaborators

The second domain of the external analysis is the organization's collaborators, including its shareholders and stakeholders. Shareholders, who own stock in a company, have a derived responsibility for the organization. Stakeholders, however, are individuals and

Table 2.1. Generic Cross-Impact Matrix for PEST Analysis.

KPIs	Political Trend or Event	Economic Trend or Event	Social Trend or Event	Technological Trend or Event
#1	Cell 1	Cell 6	Cell 11	Cell 16
#2	Cell 2	Cell 7	Cell 12	Cell 17
#3	Cell 3	Cell 8	Cell 13	Cell 18
#4	Cell 4	Cell 9	Cell 14	Cell 19
#5	Cell 5	Cell 10	Cell 15	Cell 20

Sample Scale for Rating Impact in Each Cell:
6 = strong positive influence
5 = moderate positive influence
4 = weak positive influence
3 = weak negative influence
2 = moderate negative influence
1 = strong negative influence
0 = neutral, don't know, no impact, not applicable

Table 2.2. Sample Individual PEST Cross-Impact Analysis.

KPIs	(P)New state policy: low tuition, low taxes, cut state agency budgets	(E)High unemployment	(S)Population increase in the region; birth rate increase; immigration increase	(T)Using technology to personalize instruction— 20 percent increase in grades
FTE enrollment	1	6	6	4
Tuition rate	1	0	0	0
Graduation rate	1	3	0	6
State appropriation	1	3	4	3
Financial aid	2	3	6	2

organizations who have a vested interest in the institution's success. Examples include employers, parents, students, suppliers, lenders, employee unions, special interest groups, government agencies, and professional associations. For public institutions, the state legislature and the executive branch of state government are especially important stakeholders.

The SWOT analysis of collaborators first requires identification by name of these stakeholders, followed by articulation of the KPIs that these stakeholders use to measure their own success and those they use to measure the success of the institution with which they collaborate. A cross-impact analysis of stakeholder KPIs with the institution's own KPIs allows the SPC to identify win-win scenarios, to pinpoint potential collaborations, and to recognize possible opportunities and threats to the institution. The cross-impact analysis for collaborators would be done along the same lines as the PEST analysis shown in Tables 2.1 and 2.2.

The responses that are reflected in the results of the various cross-impact analyses represent the beliefs of individuals in the SPC, and they may or may not be accurate. At this point, this is not a critical factor in making decisions; it is the aggregated data that will be used to inform decision makers.

Analysis of Competitors

The third domain studied by the external analysis is the organization's competitors. Competitors seek attention and resources from the same customers, suppliers, and providers. They are organizations that may have a negative interest in the institution carrying out the analysis. In the higher education context, competitors include other colleges or universities, usually in the same geographic area. For state institutions, however, competitors also include other entities vying for state funding: K–12 education, law enforcement, prisons, health care, and economic development, to name a few. Again, identification of these competitors is the first step in the analytical process, followed by specification of their impact on the focal institution's KPIs.

These activities can take the form of competitive market and peer group analyses. In such studies it is important to understand the programs and services offered at other campuses within the area served by the focal institution. In carrying out such studies, planners discover areas of duplication as well as areas of underserved needs. By looking at the student market, such as high school graduation trends and the preferences being expressed by this emergent student group, planners can also begin to determine the needs of future college or university students and match these needs against the institution's capacity to serve them.

In addition to identifying important competitors, this analysis helps to illuminate their strategies and tactics, and helps the SPC to develop a clearer understanding of how these practices affect the organization's own success as expressed through the KPIs identified in Step 1. Once again, the cross-impact analysis for competitors would be done along the same lines as the PEST analysis, shown in Tables 2.1 and 2.2.

The Combined External Environmental Cross-Impact Analysis

Step 2D of the strategic planning engine, shown in Figure 2.1, represents a series of cross-impact analyses that the SPC would go through. Each individual cross-impact analysis described in this chapter harvests the collective judgment of the group, focuses group discussion, and identifies necessary supporting analysis. Each illustrates a component of the matrix referred to as Step 2D.

Examining each individual's scores can stimulate interesting and provocative questions and discussions regarding what reasoning was applied to arrive at the assigned values. Why, for example, did the individual believe that the election of a new governor with a platform of low taxes and low tuition and a commitment to reduce the state budget by cutting all agencies would result in a strong positive influence on the institution's graduation rate?

Open discussion of the perceived impact of environmental factors on organizational KPIs is a very important step in preparing the SPC for effective decision making. But in order to avoid undue pressure on individual members, it is sometimes better to analyze only *group aggregate scores*. Group scores show the central

Table 2.3. Sample Group PEST Cross-Impact Analysis.

KPIs	(P) New governor's platform: low tuition, low taxes, cut state agency budgets	(E) High inflation rate and unemployment; new jobs require a college education	(S)Population increase in the region; birth rate increase; immigration increase	(T)Using technology to personalize instruction— 20 percent increase in grades
FTE enrollment	Mean 1.3 STD .34	Mean 5.55 STD .01	Mean 5.9 STD .01	Mean 5.8 STD .01
Tuition rate	Mean 1.2 STD .46	Mean 3.2 STD .01	Mean 4.2 STD .01	Mean 2.3 STD .01
Graduation rate	Mean 0.9 STD 3.11	Mean 2.1 STD 1.01	Mean 2.6 STD 3.7	Mean 5.1 STD 1.51
State appropriation	Mean 1.4 STD .02	Mean 1.8 STD .01	Mean 3.7 STD 2.84	Mean 2.8 STD .26
Financial aid	Mean 2.1 STD .01	Mean 2.1 STD .01	Mean 3.3 STD 1.72	Mean 3.4 STD .32

tendencies of the group and save individuals from being put on the spot to justify responses. In either event, the analysis of the results of the cross-impact analyses is a useful tool toward this end.

Table 2.3 provides an example of the means and standard deviations for aggregate scores of a group of individuals filling in Table 2.2. The mean indicates the average group response and the standard deviation indicates the level of consensus. The higher the standard deviation, the more widely spread the group members' individual judgments. High standard deviations reveal that more discussion may be needed to develop greater consensus. The cross-impact analysis group scores can also be derived by public group discussion with a facilitator seeking verbal consensus. This approach may not work well in groups composed of members of unequal status. In such cases, a variety of techniques, such as computer-based decision support process or electronic voting pads, can be used to eliminate status barriers by masking the identity of the individual and counting everyone's vote equally.

Identification of Opportunities and Threats

The systematic evaluation of the external environment serves to identify opportunities that might help the institution achieve its goals, as well as identifying specific external threats to organizational success. These opportunities should be carefully articulated and defined using the output from the cross-impact analyses. When the external environmental analysis is complete and the threats and opportunities are clearly identified, the SPC can now turn its attention to an analysis of the internal environment.

Outcomes

Once the SPC has identified the most important of the institution's external constituencies and forces, it will have learned to discern between those external elements that the college or university can control and those that it cannot. This is essential information. Because the central point of strategic planning is to align the institution with its environment, this knowledge allows the SPC to choose the types of strategies and goals that will position the institution to maximize its linkage to the external world and take advantage of its most important opportunities. This analysis is particularly important for the public institution because it addresses the fit between what the institution is and what its public constituents expect from it.

Hints

1. The governing board represents a key external constituent. The beliefs and interests of its members must be considered in order for this part of the analysis to be realistic.

2. Donors are another group that must be taken into account. They are a growing source of financial support, and they influence what can be done to put a plan into operation.

3. Excellence, quality, and related notions that are defined by external constituents cannot be overlooked as the campus defines these same elements internally. Any dissonance is likely to be evident in public rejection.

4. The use of an outside consultant to conduct a more intensive search of public perceptions and provide a more objective assessment of the results might prove useful here. Those on the inside may well not be as objective about how the institution is viewed by the public, and an outside expert will usually provide valuable information that could not otherwise be collected.

5. A scan of the external environment has the potential for identifying unique niches between public desires and the institution's internal capabilities. This information is especially important to use as a guide when mission is reviewed or modified. Ideas about mission can be made more practical based on this analysis.

6.   Keep the working list short. The world is a big place, and there are lots of influences that one could add to this analysis. This will not be helpful. Rather, ask, Is this item absolutely necessary as a descriptor of what strategically impacts this institution? This will help eliminate those forces that do not directly impact the focal college or university, and it will provide a much more relevant and effective list of opportunities and threats that the institution should address.

7.   Keep the process short. Academics love to analyze comprehensively. Planners must think strategically. What is needed here is a listing of the most important environmental forces, which usually show up early in the analysis. If allowed to, this part of the process could add literally months to the planning exercise and add little to what was identified in the first few meetings.

Worksheets

There are three sets of worksheets in this section. The first set will help the individual participant and the group to identify the most important forces, elements, or events that comprise its most important external environmental set (the political, economic, sociological, technical, collaborative, and competitive forces). The second set may be used first by individuals to conduct a series of cross-impact analyses, then by the group to produce summaries. The third set of worksheets results from the other two and constitutes the working set of opportunities and threats that the planning group will use to develop strategies to take best advantage of future possibilities. Participants using a decision support center should fill out worksheets 2.1, 2.2, and 2.3 prior to attending the session in which the planning group will evaluate external forces. Participants using spreadsheet templates will find corresponding template files under "Step2" and "CrossImA" on the disk of spreadsheet templates.

Worksheets 2.1 through 2.6 take participants and groups through the identification, collection, and prioritization of the most important external factors that affect the institution. For those using the paper forms method, go through the individual forms first and then meet as a group to collect everyone's data, refine it, and prioritize it using brainstorming techniques. For those using the decision support center, group work can include collecting, organizing, and voting on priority lists for each of the six categories. For those using the spreadsheet method, the spreadsheets available can be used to collect, organize, and set up a paper vote for prioritizing final working lists.

The cross-impact analyses will differ based on the method each group is using. For the decision support center users, the matrix analytical tool sets up the data along a row and column configuration, collects individual data input, and provides a wide variety of statistical data for helping to interpret the results. Spreadsheet users will find a set of instructions at the beginning of the spreadsheet files on the disk that will provide two different methods of entering and collecting data; these users should refer to the disk for further instructions. Users of the paper forms will find forms for each of the six analyses in the following pages of the workbook (Worksheets 2.7 through 2.12). Each participant will manually add the working list of KPIs to each form, and then add the working lists that have come from the work done on Worksheets 2.1 through 2.6 as directed on the forms. Calculating results by hand will take some time. Each matrix cell should be calculated based on the input of all participants (in other words, when calculating the results of the input on the matrix cell that measures the impact of the first political factor on the first KPI, the numbers from each participant should be calculated together). Typical output is a mean and standard deviation for each cell, and should be reported on a paper report form (not provided in this workbook).

Interpretation of the data results from any method is left up to the discretion of each group. In general, however, high mean numbers indicate a strong effect relationship, and the standard deviation can indicate the level of agreement that exists among the participants. Looking over the entire set of outcomes will reveal trends, which the group can conclude indicate that particular external factors are more important than others in their effect on the institution. This knowledge then allows the group to construct the final two lists involved in this step—the listing of opportunities and threats. Use Worksheets 2.13 and 2.14 to list those opportunities and threats that participants feel will have the greatest effect upon the college or university.

Identification of Political and Economic Forces

Before the group meeting in which the SPC will identify, discuss, analyze, and prioritize the external elements of the college or university that have the most important effects on the institution, each participant should develop her or his own list. Use this form to list those political and economic forces that you believe presently have or potentially will have an impact on your college or university.

Political forces that do (or could) affect the institution:

1.

2.

3.

4.

5.

6.

7.

8.

Economic forces that do (or could) affect the institution:

1.

2.

3.

4.

5.

6.

7.

8.

WORKSHEET 2.2 Individual

Identification of Sociological and Technical Forces

Before the group meeting in which the SPC will identify, discuss, analyze, and prioritize those external elements of the college or university that have the most important effects on the institution, each participant should develop her or his own list. Use this form to list those sociological and technical forces that you believe presently have or potentially will have impact on your college or university.

Sociological forces that do (or could) affect the institution:

1.

2.

3.

4.

5.

6.

7.

8.

Technical forces that do (or could) affect the institution:

1.

2.

3.

4.

5.

6.

7.

8.

Identification of Collaborative and Competitive Forces

Before the group meeting in which the SPC will identify, discuss, analyze, and prioritize those external elements of the college or university that have the most important effects on the institution, each participant should develop her or his own list. Use this form to list those collaborative and competitive forces that you believe presently have or potential will have an impact on your college or university.

Collaborative forces that do (or could) affect the institution:

1.

2.

3.

4.

5.

6.

7.

8.

Competitive forces that do (or could) affect the institution:

1.

2.

3.

4.

5.

6.

7.

8.

WORKSHEET 2.4   Group
_____

Prioritization of Political and Economic Forces

Once the group has identified, discussed, and analyzed a list of political and economic forces using brainstorming techniques, it must then prioritize these external elements of the college or university to determine the most important items. The top items will be used to help develop the institution's strategic plan. We suggest that you identify only the top eight items, though you may choose to identify more. After the group's discussion, the list here should represent your final set.

Political forces that do (or could) affect the institution:

1.

2.

3.

4.

5.

6.

7.

8.

Economic forces that do (or could) affect the institution:

1.

2.

3.

4.

5.

6.

7.

8.

Prioritization of Sociological and Technical Forces

Once the group has identified, discussed, and analyzed a list of sociological and technical forces using brainstorming techniques, it must then prioritize the external elements of the college or university to determine the most important items. These top items will be used to help develop the institution's strategic plan. We suggest that you identify only the top eight items, though you may choose to identify more. After the group's discussion, the list here should represent your final set.

Sociological forces that do (or could) affect the institution:

1.

2.

3.

4.

5.

6.

7.

8.

Technical forces that do (or could) affect the institution:

1.

2.

3.

4.

5.

6.

7.

8.

WORKSHEET 2.6   Group
_____

Prioritization of Collaborative and Competitive Forces

Once the group has identified, discussed, and analyzed a list of collaborative and competitive forces using brainstorming techniques, it must then prioritize these external elements of the college or university to determine the most important items. These top items will be used to help develop the institution's strategic plan. We suggest that you identify only the top eight items, though you may choose to identify more. After the group's discussion, the list here should represent your final set.

Collaborative forces that do (or could) affect the institution:

1.
2.
3.
4.
5.
6.
7.
8.

Competitive forces that do (or could) affect the institution:

1.
2.
3.
4.
5.
6.
7.
8.

Cross-Impact Analysis: Effects of Political Forces on KPIs

List the group's final set of political forces in the top column spaces and the working list of KPIs in the left-hand row spaces. Then, indicate in the intersecting spaces what you believe to be the effect of the political force on the KPIs. Use the following scale, or use a scale with which the group feels more comfortable.

6 = strong positive influence
5 = moderate positive influence
4 = weak positive influence
3 = weak negative influence

2 = moderate negative influence
1 = strong negative influence
0 = neutral, don't know, no impact,
    not applicable

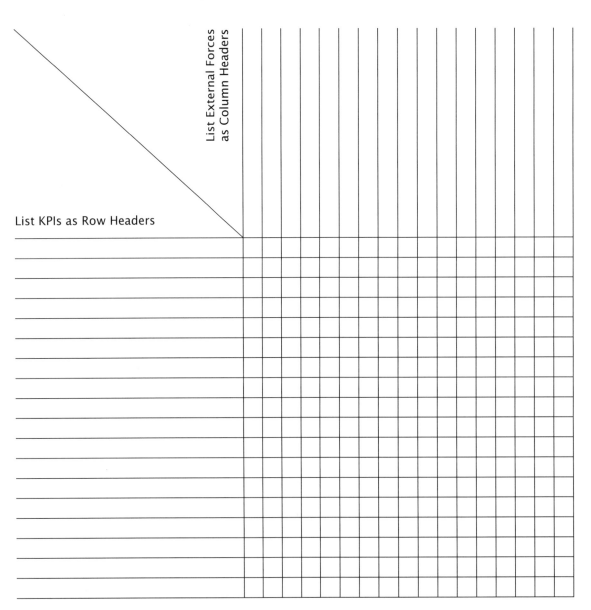

List External Forces as Column Headers

List KPIs as Row Headers

WORKSHEET 2.8   Individual

Cross-Impact Analysis: Effects of Economic Forces on KPIs

List the group's final set of economic forces in the top column spaces and the working list of KPIs in the left-hand row spaces. Then indicate in the intersecting space what you believe to be the effect of the economic forces on the KPIs. Use the following scale, or use a scale with which the group feels more comfortable.

6 = strong positive influence   2 = moderate negative influence
5 = moderate positive influence   1 = strong negative influence
4 = weak positive influence   0 = neutral, don't know, no impact,
3 = weak negative influence   not applicable

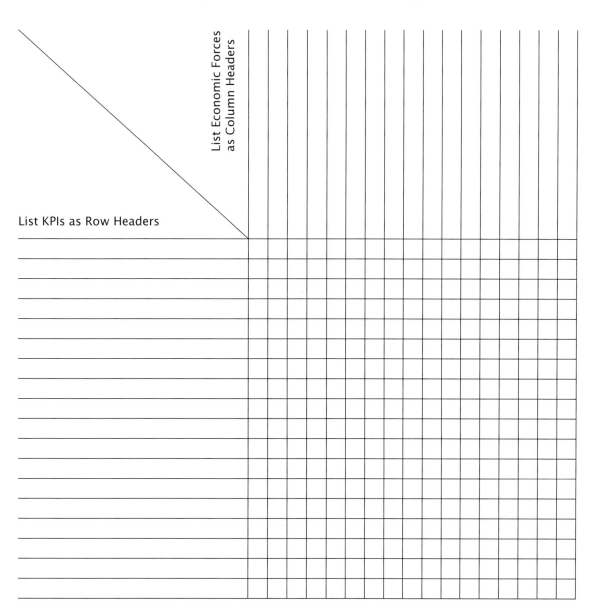

List Economic Forces as Column Headers

List KPIs as Row Headers

Cross-Impact Analysis: Effects of Sociological Forces on KPIs

List the group's final set of sociological forces in the top column spaces and the working list of KPIs in the left-hand row spaces. Then indicate in the intersecting space what you believe to be the effect of the sociological forces on the KPIs. Use the following scale, or use a scale with which the group feels more comfortable.

6 = strong positive influence   2 = moderate negative influence
5 = moderate positive influence   1 = strong negative influence
4 = weak positive influence   0 = neutral, don't know, no impact,
3 = weak negative influence   not applicable

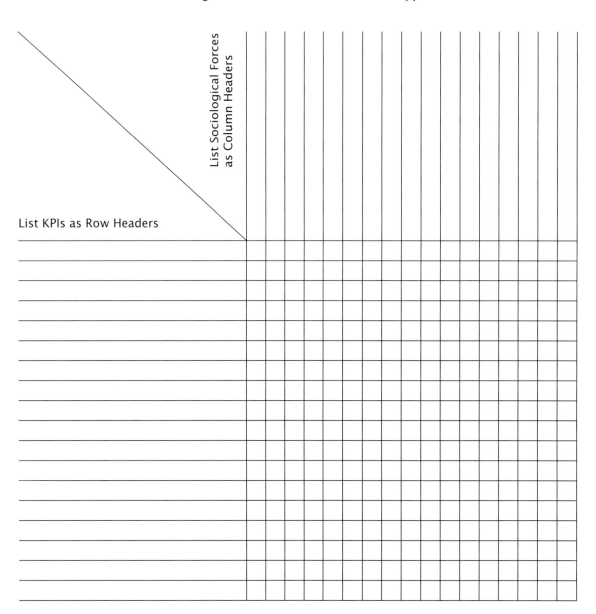

List Sociological Forces as Column Headers

List KPIs as Row Headers

WORKSHEET 2.10 Individual

Cross-Impact Analysis: Effects of Technical Forces on KPIs

List the group's final set of technical forces in the top column spaces and the working list of KPIs in the left-hand row spaces. Then indicate in the intersecting spaces what you believe to be the effect of the technical forces on the KPIs. Use the following scale, or use a scale with which the group feels more comfortable.

6 = strong positive influence   2 = moderate negative influence
5 = moderate positive influence   1 = strong negative influence
4 = weak positive influence   0 = neutral, don't know, no impact,
3 = weak negative influence   not applicable

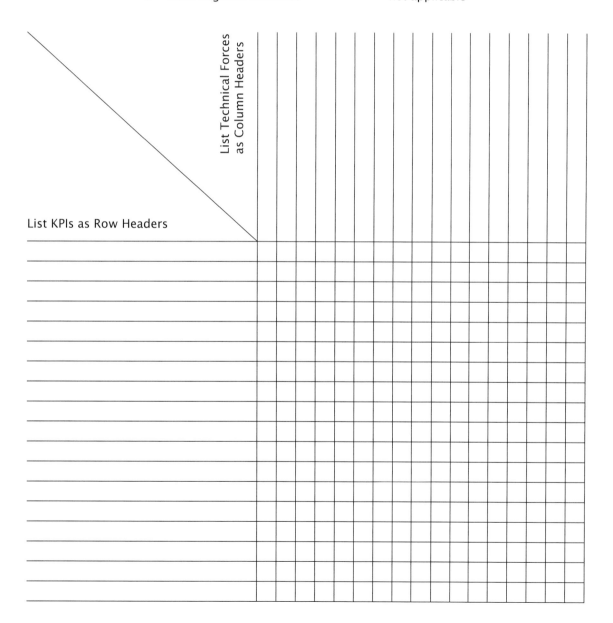

List Technical Forces as Column Headers

List KPIs as Row Headers

Cross-Impact Analysis: Effects of Collaborative Forces on KPIs

List the group's final set of collaborative forces in the top column spaces and the working list of KPIs in the left-hand row spaces. Then indicate in the intersecting spaces what you believe to be the effect of the collaborative forces on the KPI. Use the following scale, or use a scale with which the group feels more comfortable.

6 = strong positive influence   2 = moderate negative influence
5 = moderate positive influence   1 = strong negative influence
4 = weak positive influence   0 = neutral, don't know, no impact,
3 = weak negative influence   not applicable

List Collaborative Forces as Column Headers

List KPIs as Row Headers

WORKSHEET 2.12   Individual

Cross-Impact Analysis: Effects of Competitive Forces on KPIS

List the group's final set of competitive forces in the top column spaces and the working list of KPIs in the left-hand row spaces. Then indicate in the intersecting spaces what you believe to be the effect of the competitive force on the KPI. Use the following scale, or use a scale with which the group feels more comfortable.

6 = strong positive influence   2 = moderate negative influence
5 = moderate positive influence   1 = strong negative influence
4 = weak positive influence   0 = neutral, don't know, no impact,
3 = weak negative influence   not applicable

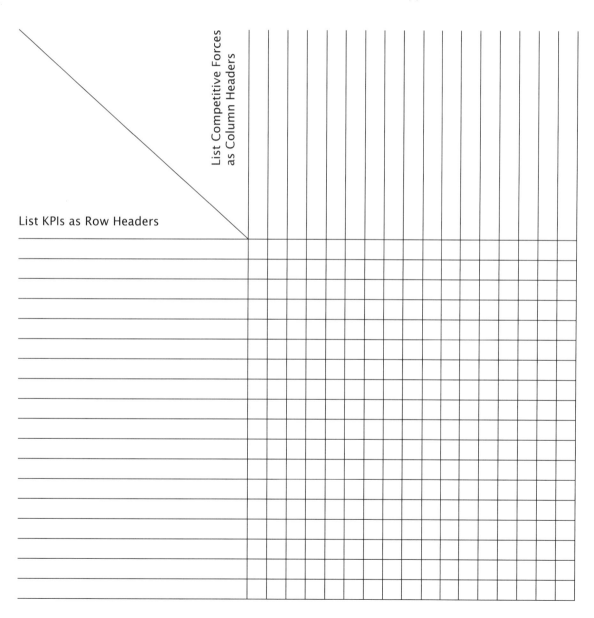

WORKSHEET 2.13   Group

Listing of Relevant Opportunities

As a result of the several cross-impact analysis exercises your group has conducted, the SPC should now translate the results of the several PEST, collaborator, and competitor analyses by identifying the most promising opportunities that the several analyses suggest. Conduct the group exercise using the general rules of brainstorming, as before, and write the top several opportunities in the space below. Sort the group choices based on the KPI classification areas. (Opportunities are those things that the college or university could do to improve its fit with the external environment.)

Top Opportunities:

Academic:

1.

2.

3.

Enrollments:

1.
2.
3.

Administrative:

1.

2.

3.

Resources:

1.

2.

3.

Campus support:

1.

2.

3.

Information technology:

1.

2.

3.

Other:

1.

2.

3.

WORKSHEET 2.14   Group

Listing of Important Threats

Again, as a result of the several cross-impact analysis exercises your group has conducted, the SPC should now translate the results of the several PEST, collaborator, and competitor analyses by identifying the most important threats that the several analyses suggest. Conduct the group exercise using the general rules of brainstorming, as before, and write the top several threats in the space below. Sort the group choices based on the KPI classification areas. (Threats are conditions, happenings, or situations external to the institution that can negatively affect the institution or prevent it from pursuing its opportunities.)

Top Threats:

Academic:

1.

2.

3.

Enrollments:

1.
2.
3.

Administrative:

1.

2.

3.

Resources:

1.

2.

3.

Campus support:

1.

2.

3.

Information technology:

1.

2.

3.

Other:

1.

2.

3.

Assessing the Internal Environment

With the development of the external analysis now in focus, it is time to look at the internal environment of the college or university. What the strategic planning committee (SPC) is trying to determine is the ability of the institution to take advantage of its most important opportunities while minimizing the effects of, or avoiding altogether, the various threats that can create problems as the institution heads toward its long-term goals. The internal analysis identifies the college's or university's most important assets, events, traditions, and activities (its strengths) and its most important limiting characteristics (its weaknesses), which the SPC will document in this step as those items that the institution can or cannot use in developing its strategic plan.

The SWOT analysis of the internal environment should focus on identifying (1) the areas of excellence the college or university has been able to build and maintain, (2) the resources it has at its disposal, (3) where those resources come from, (4) its high-demand programs and services, (5) the quality of its human resources, (6) its academic tradition, (7) the internal political realities of the campus, and (8) the quality and strength of its leadership and governance structures. Such an analysis will lead to the development of two lists—the major *strengths* and the most prominent *weaknesses* that exist on the campus (or within the college or university system).

To be useful, the analysis needs to be as factual as possible, and to carefully avoid impressions and speculation. As a result, these two lists become a simplified snapshot of what the institution is at one point in time, and they also help to put bounds on what

Figure 3.1.
Strategic Planning Engine Step 3.

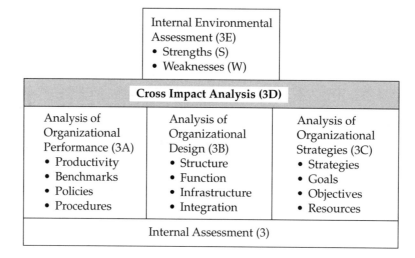

the campus is capable of accomplishing and what it is not. While this may not always be comforting to know, it is crucial for successful strategic planning.

The purpose of the internal assessment is to evaluate the influence that organizational design, performance, strategies, goals, objectives, and resources have on achieving KPIs. Organizational units tend to use this type of review to make the case for more resources. This tendency should be avoided during this stage of the planning process. The analysis should be taken as an opportunity to describe the current state of the institution as a baseline. It includes assessments of three interrelated components: organizational performance, organizational design, and organizational strategies. These are detailed in sections 3A, 3B, and 3C of the strategic planning engine model (see Figure 3.1).

Analysis of Organizational Performance

The analysis of current performance includes an evaluation of productivity, benchmarks, and organizational policies and procedures. The first step is to define productivity. This definition is then used to evaluate the extent to which the KPIs articulated in Step 1 capture productivity measures so they can be evaluated. The next step is to establish benchmarks. These can be the average performance metrics of similar institutions, the performance levels of competitors, or a compilation of the best practices in the industry. Benchmarks help anchor the internal analysis in performance standards that are set closely in line with external expectations.

Table 3.1. Sample Individual Cross-Impact Matrix for Policies and Procedures.

KPIs	*Academic advising is under three Vice Presidential jurisdictions*	*Information-technology is under three Vice Presidential jurisdictions*	*Academic Program Development does not include Service Units*	*Recruitment and Retention Responsibility is shared by 22 different offices*
FTE enrollment	2	1	2	2
Tuition rate	0	2	3	3
Graduation rate	4	0	0	0
State appropriation	3	0	9	0
Financial aid	0	4	5	6

Colleges and universities can only achieve progress toward the desired values for the organization's KPIs if organizational policies and procedures facilitate their realization. Ultimately, every organizational policy and procedure should be passed through a cross-impact analysis, with their impact measured against the organization's KPIs. In this way, the SPC can also assess the impact of each policy on benchmarks and productivity measures. A policy-and-procedure cross-impact analysis can be conducted immediately; it provides a crisp vision of how current operations affect organizational performance.

A great deal of discussion is generated by such a review. As is evident from the examples in Table 3.1, the interpretation of each cross-impact is case specific. Results pinpoint aggregate group thinking, which forces the group to carefully articulate the purpose of the policy or procedure and deal with its impact on the organization's key performance indicators (KPIs). During the analysis of organizational performance, the SPC should review major policies and procedures in this way.

Analysis of Organizational Design

In this part of the analysis, the SPC will evaluate four components of organizational design: structure, function, infrastructure, and integration. The purpose of this analysis is to gain insight into the impact of organizational design on KPIs. For the purposes of this discussion, we define structure as the authority, governance, and reporting relationships that establish rules of operation within an organization. Structure is often diagramed in organizational charts and classified into hierarchical, flat, star, or other organizational typologies. When structure is combined with division, unit, and individual functions and analyzed against organizational KPIs, some interesting insights begin to emerge. Again, the group can discover these insights through the use of the cross-impact analysis, in the same manner as shown in Table 3.1. For example, it could be found that hierarchical, function-based organizational structures retard the achievement of KPI targets for enrollment and retention of students.

Just as important as an analysis of structure and function is an analysis of organization infrastructure. Such an analysis should include a consideration of the physical plant, telecommunication networks, administrative and academic information systems, and classroom equipment. The final dimension of organizational design that needs to be analyzed is how well the different divisions, units, and even individuals integrate their activity and efforts. This analysis should include judgments on the levels of cross-unit integration and communication within the organization.

Analysis of Current Organizational Strategies

The SPC should next articulate the organization's present strategies, goals, objectives, tactics, and resources. This activity should be done through the lenses of both the KPIs and the previously determined benchmark and productivity measures. Strategies are, or should be, long-term in nature, although they may have significant short-term impact on the organization, its collaborators, and its competitors. Resources are the fiscal, human, technological, and organizational inputs to the organization's operations. Once again, the SPC should conduct a cross-impact analysis, as illustrated in Table 3.1, to evaluate the impact of current strategies, goals, objectives, and fiscal and human resources on the achievement of organizational KPIs.

Internal Assessment Cross-Impact Analysis

Step 3D of the strategic planning engine model, illustrated in Figure 3.1, represents a series of cross-impact analyses of the internal environmental set. Each component cross-impact analysis harvests the collective judgment of the group, focuses group discussion, and identifies necessary supporting analysis. For the external assessment, SWOT analysis is conducted using a two-dimensional matrix in which the organization's KPIs are arrayed down the rows and the factors to be evaluated for impact on KPIs are arrayed across the columns.

Identification of Strengths and Weaknesses _____

The systematic evaluation of the internal environment serves to identify specific strengths and weaknesses of the organization. They should be carefully articulated and defined using the output from the cross-impact analyses. With the internal environmental analysis complete and the strengths and weaknesses clearly identified, attention is turned to an analysis of both the external and internal environment on organizational KPIs.

Outcomes _____

Following the completion of this step, the planning group will have a more focused idea about who and what the college or university is all about. This can be a sobering as well as rewarding experience. On the one hand, no institution is perfect—every organization has flaws that it tends to overlook, or at least to play down, as it performs its day-to-day and long-term activities. These flaws might be insignificant in the grander scheme of things, or they could be clear detriments to the college's or university's moving forward in the direction that is best for it. On the other hand, every institution has assets and positive qualities that often go unnoticed or unused. Beyond the assets the planning committee will already be aware of, these otherwise hidden assets often provide a necessary edge for the organization as its seeks to move ahead. By taking the time to become better acquainted with its internal assets and flaws, the planning group will have developed a more objective sense of who and what the institution is and what it is capable of doing. This knowledge will be very helpful in the next few steps of the process of developing a comprehensive, focused, reasonable, and effective strategic plan.

Hints _____

1. It is often hard for individuals or groups to be objective about themselves or about their college or university. This is one of the advantages of the brainstorming method of group decision making. By having individuals prepare their own lists ahead of time and then creating a master group list, first without comment (until the list is complete) and then by an objective group discussion about the various items, the group will achieve a more objective view.

2. The cross-impact analysis that analyzes the effects of col-

lege or university policy on KPIs is usually an especially effective exercise in demonstrating the power of environmental forces on both key performance areas and their outcomes. This lesson usually also demonstrates the robust strength of the cross-impact analysis tool.

3. In order to gain a comprehensive internal perspective, it is advisable that a widely representative group of campus people be involved in developing the information required for this step. This might be done by establishing a short-term task force that includes people from every segment of the campus, or by using a campus survey instrument. Gathering data in this fashion will help the SPC establish a more realistic view of campus assets and failings than they could gain from their own experiences and inputs alone.

4. External constituents can prove to be an effective secondary source of information, but the SPC should select carefully who they would like to involve—not everyone outside the institution is either knowledgeable or objective about the internal realities of the campus. However, program reviews, accreditation reports, consultants' opinions, alumni surveys, interviews of governing board members, community leaders' views, report of employers of graduates, and the opinions of major providers of funds all help provide an additional sense of institutional strengths and weaknesses.

5. Keep the process to a short time frame. As in the external analysis, it is possible to spend so much time gathering data that the process can lose momentum and support. Further, usually the most important items will come out early in any event, and taking more time to try to discover more in-depth information may prove to be a waste of time.

6. Use the results of the various data collection methods as the basis for individual members to begin their lists, beginning with Worksheet 3.1. Also, encourage group members to feel free to add their own ideas and not feel bound by the data sets developed outside the committee.

7. Beware of "groupthink." Avoid discussions of competitors and the "us versus them" that can sneak into this particular analysis. Objectivity is the key to success here.

Worksheets

The worksheets that the group should use in this step are similar to those that were involved in the previous step. The process for using them is also similar. This will be true for those groups using a decision support center, the spreadsheet templates, or the paper forms method. Those wishing to use the spreadsheet templates will find them on the disk in the file labeled "Step3."

The first activity will be to gather data about the internal pluses and minuses that make up the reality of the campus. As indicated in Worksheets 3.1, 3.2, and 3.3, there are several specific areas from which we recommend that data should be gathered. Depending on the time and resources available to the strategic planning group, you may decide to use all, some, or none of the suggestions provided in the hints the authors have provided in this chapter. But regardless of whether you use internal task forces and external reports to help gather your data, or whether you find that you must depend on the collective wisdom of the members of the SPC, encourage thoughtful research and data collection based on the categories you find in the worksheets. Please note that these lists should be sensitive only to the categories on the list, *not to whether the items are positive or negative.* Both positive and negative items should be included at this point.

Once the group has received its reports and/or has determined how it will have members prepare themselves, each member should complete Worksheets 3.1, 3.2, and 3.3 as homework. Those groups using the decision support center or the paper forms method should do this. Those groups using the spreadsheet templates will find on the disk individual templates for this purpose.

When the group meets to work on this step together, it will use the examples found on Worksheets 3.4, 3.5, and 3.6 to gather, organize, and prioritize its several lists of internal environmental items. Again, the group should not be worried at this point about whether the items are positive or negative, but only about whether or not the items fit the categories properly. Using brainstorming methods, the group should organize and prioritize each categorical list, arriving at a point where it will select the top items to carry forward as its working list.

Those using the decision support center can use programs available to categorize and to prioritize by one of the voting choices available. Those using the spreadsheet templates can move items around on their cumulative spreadsheets to categorize more accurately, and then conduct a vote on paper ballot to prioritize. Those using the paper forms method will use either a blackboard or a presentation tablet to develop group lists, and then do a paper ballot to help determine a proper prioritization.

After the group has prioritized the items on the several lists, then it will use the cross-impact analysis tools described in Step 2 to analyze each of the most important internal items against the list of KPIs the group established in Step 1. This analysis will help establish which of the internal items have a major effect on the KPIs, which will help the group further refine their working lists.

The final part of this step is to review the surviving list of internal items and then categorize the items into the most important strengths and weaknesses that could have a strategic effect on the planning process of the college or university. Now it is time to look at the positive and negative effects of the items and put the surviving positive items on the list in Worksheet 3.14 of the institution's most important strengths, and the surviving negative items on the list in Worksheet 3.15 of the institution's most important weaknesses. Add each strength and weakness to the appropriate list by also indicating which KPI it fits under. Again, use brainstorming techniques to complete this function. The paper form groups will use the lists they have already developed to create these last two lists; the decision support center groups can use a program that categorizes data to perform this task; and the spreadsheet template groups can combine results of previous steps onto specific templates on the master disk to identify strengths and weaknesses.

WORKSHEET 3.1   Individual

Identification of Organizational Performance

Before the group meeting in which the SPC will identify, discuss, analyze, and prioritize the internal elements of the college or university that have the most important effects on its performance, each participant should develop her or his own list. Use this form to list those major elements of performance (in the categories listed below) that you believe presently have or potentially will have an impact on your college or university. Include both positive and negative items in your list.

Internal politics that do (or could) affect the institution:

1.

2.

3.

4.

5.

6.

7.

8.

Academic traditions that do (or could) affect the institution:

1.

2.

3.

4.

5.

6.

7.

8.

Policies that do (or could) affect the institution:

1.

2.

3.

4.

5.

6.

7.

8.

Procedures that do (or could) affect the institution:

1.

2.

3.

4.

5.

6.

7.

8.

*Current organizational strategies that do (or could) affect
the institution:*

1.

2.

3.

4.

5.

6.

7.

8.

WORKSHEET 3.2   Individual

Identification of Organizational Design

As in Worksheet 3.1, before the group meeting in which the SPC will identify, discuss, analyze, and prioritize the internal elements of the college or university that have the most important effects on its performance, each participant should develop her or his own list. Use this form to list those major elements of organizational design (in the categories listed below) that you believe presently have or potentially could have an impact on your college or university. Include both positive and negative items in your list.

Leadership factors that do (or could) affect the institution:

1.

2.

3.

4.

5.

6.

7.

8.

Governance factors that do (or could) affect the institution:

1.

2.

3.

4.

5.

6.

7.

8.

WORKSHEET 3.2 *continued*

*Current goals (long-term) that do (or could) affect
the institution:*

1.

2.

3.

4.

5.

6.

7.

8.

*Current objectives (short-term) that do (or could) affect
the institution:*

1.

2.

3.

4.

5.

6.

7.

8.

WORKSHEET 3.3   Individual

Identification of Resource Bases

As in Worksheets 3.1 and 3.2, before the group meeting in which the SPC will identify, discuss, analyze, and prioritize the internal elements of the college or university that have the most important effects on its performance, each participant should develop her or his own list. Use this form to list those resource bases (in the categories listed below) that you believe presently have or potentially could have an impact on your college or university. Include both positive and negative items in your list.

Areas of excellence that do (or could) affect the institution:

1.

2.

3.

4.

5.

6.

7.

8.

High-demand programs and services that do (or could) affect the institution:

1.

2.

3.

4.

5.

6.

7.

8.

Areas of poor quality that do (or could) affect the institution:

1.
2.
3.
4.
5.
6.
7.
8.

Low-demand programs and services that do (or could) affect the institution:

1.
2.
3.
4.
5.
6.
7.
8.

Fiscal and capital resource qualities that do (or could) affect the institution:

1.
2.
3.
4.
5.
6.
7.
8.

WORKSHEET 3.3   *continued*

Human resources qualities that do (or could) affect the institution:

1.

2.

3.

4.

5.

6.

7.

8.

Selection of Organizational Performance Items

After the group has collected organizational performance items from participants (Worksheet 3.1) using brainstorming techniques, it must then analyze these items to determine which ones are the most important. These top items will be used to develop the institution's strategic plan. We suggest that you identify only the top eight items, though you may choose to identify more. Include both positive and negative items on your list. After the group's discussion, the list here should represent your final set.

Internal politics that do (or could) affect the institution:

1.

2.

3.

4.

5.

6.

7.

8.

Academic traditions that do (or could) affect the institution:

1.

2.

3.

4.

5.

6.

7.

8.

WORKSHEET 3.4 *continued*

Policies that do (or could) affect the institution:

1.

2.

3.

4.

5.

6.

7.

8.

Procedures that do (or could) affect the institution:

1.

2.

3.

4.

5.

6.

7.

8.

Current organizational strategies that do (or could) affect the institution:

1.

2.

3.

4.

5.

6.

7.

8.

Selection of Organizational Design Items

After the group has collected organizational design items from participants (Worksheet 3.2) using brainstorming techniques, it must then analyze these items to determine which ones are the most important. These top items will be used to help develop the institution's strategic plan. We suggest that you identify only the top eight items, though you may choose to identify more. Include both positive and negative items on your list. After the group's discussion, the list here should represent your final set.

Leadership factors that do (or could) affect the institution:

1.

2.

3.

4.

5.

6.

7.

8.

Governance factors that do (or could) affect the institution:

1.

2.

3.

4.

5.

6.

7.

8.

WORKSHEET 3.5   *continued*

*Current goals (long-term) that do (or could) affect
the institution:*

1.

2.

3.

4.

5.

6.

7.

8.

*Current objectives (short-term) that do (or could) affect
the institution:*

1.

2.

3.

4.

5.

6.

7.

8.

WORKSHEET 3.6   Group

Selection of Organizational Resource Bases

After the group has collected organizational resource base items from participants (Worksheet 3.3) using brainstorming techniques, it must then analyze
these items to determine which ones are the most important. These top items
will be used to help develop the institution's strategic plan. We suggest that
you identify only the top eight items, though you may choose to identify more.
Include both positive and negative items in your list. After the group's discussion, the list here should represent your final set.

Areas of excellence that do (or could) affect the institution:

1.

2.

3.

4.

5.

6.

7.

8.

High-demand programs and services that do (or could) affect the institution:

1.

2.

3.

4.

5.

6.

7.

8.

WORKSHEET 3.6 *continued*

Areas of poor quality that do (or could) affect the institution:

1.

2.

3.

4.

5.

6.

7.

8.

Low-demand programs and services that do (or could) affect the institution:

1.

2.

3.

4.

5.

6.

7.

8.

Fiscal and capital resource qualities that do (or could) affect the institution:

1.

2.

3.

4.

5.

6.

7.

8.

Human resources qualities that do (or could) affect the institution:

1.

2.

3.

4.

5.

6.

7.

8.

WORKSHEET 3.7 Individual

Cross-Impact Analysis: Organizational Performance Effects on KPIs

List the group's final set of internal political and academic traditions in the top column spaces and the working list of KPIs in the left-hand row spaces. Then indicate in the intersecting spaces what you believe to be the effect of the internal political or academic tradition upon the KPIs. Use the following scale, or use a scale with which the group feels more comfortable.

6 = strong positive influence
5 = moderate positive influence
4 = weak positive influence
3 = weak negative influence

2 = moderate negative influence
1 = strong negative influence
0 = neutral, don't know, no impact, not applicable

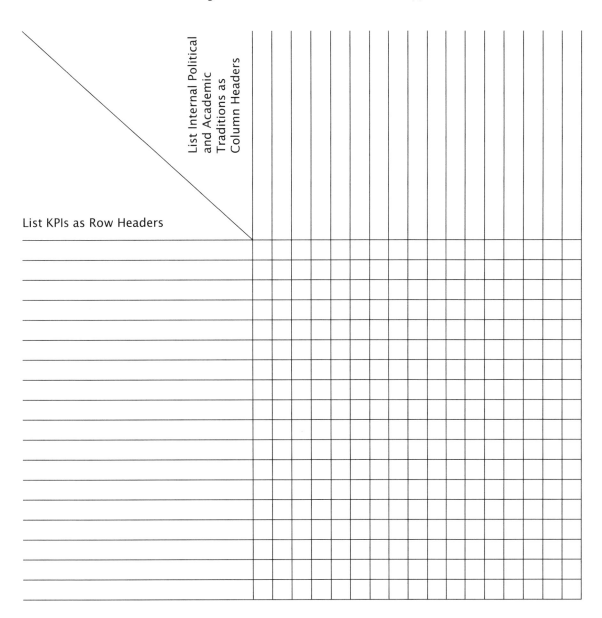

List Internal Political and Academic Traditions as Column Headers

List KPIs as Row Headers

WORKSHEET 3.8   Individual

Cross-Impact Analysis: Organizational Performance Effects on KPIs (Continued)

List the group's final set of internal policies, procedures, and current strategies in the top column spaces and the working list of KPIs in the left-hand row spaces. Then indicate in the intersecting spaces what you believe to be the effect of the policies, procedures. and current strategies upon the KPI. Use the following scale, or use a scale with which the group feels more comfortable.

6 = strong positive influence   2 = moderate negative influence
5 = moderate positive influence   1 = strong negative influence
4 = weak positive influence   0 = neutral, don't know, no impact,
3 = weak negative influence   not applicable

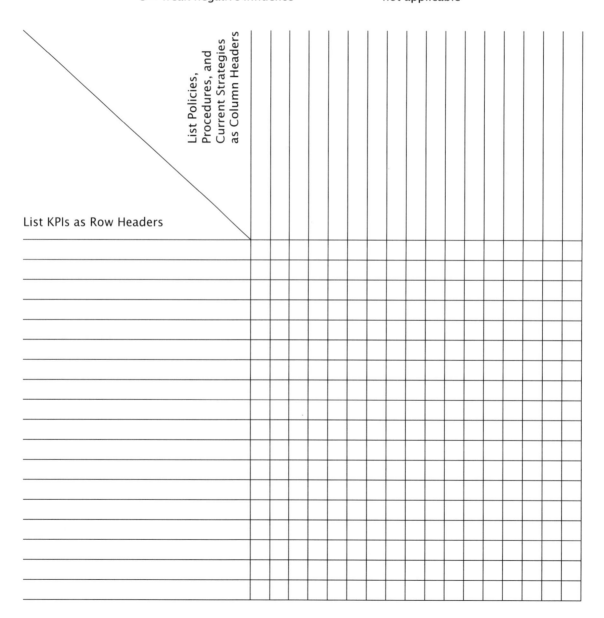

List Policies, Procedures, and Current Strategies as Column Headers

List KPIs as Row Headers

WORKSHEET 3.9   Individual

Cross-Impact Analysis: Organizational Design Effects on KPIs

List the group's final set of leadership and governance items along the top column spaces and the working list of KPIs in the left-hand row spaces. Then indicate in the intersecting spaces what you believe to be the effect of leadership and governance items on the KPI. Use the following scale, or use a scale with which the group feels more comfortable.

6 = strong positive influence   2 = moderate negative influence
5 = moderate positive influence   1 = strong negative influence
4 = weak positive influence   0 = neutral, don't know, no impact,
3 = weak negative influence   not applicable

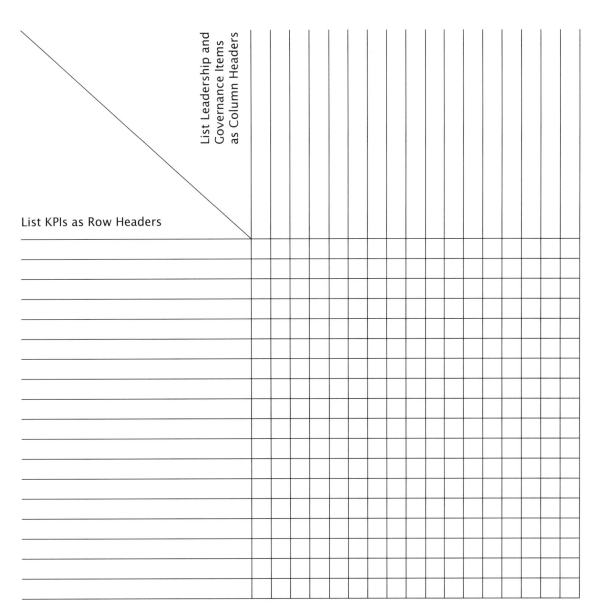

Cross-Impact Analysis: Organizational Design Effects on KPIs (Continued)

List the group's final set of current goals and objectives in the top column spaces and the working list of KPIs in the left-hand row spaces. Then indicate in the intersecting spaces what you believe to be the effect of current goals and objectives on the KPIs. Use the following scale, or use a scale with which the group feels more comfortable.

6 = strong positive influence   2 = moderate negative influence
5 = moderate positive influence   1 = strong negative influence
4 = weak positive influence   0 = neutral, don't know, no impact,
3 = weak negative influence   not applicable

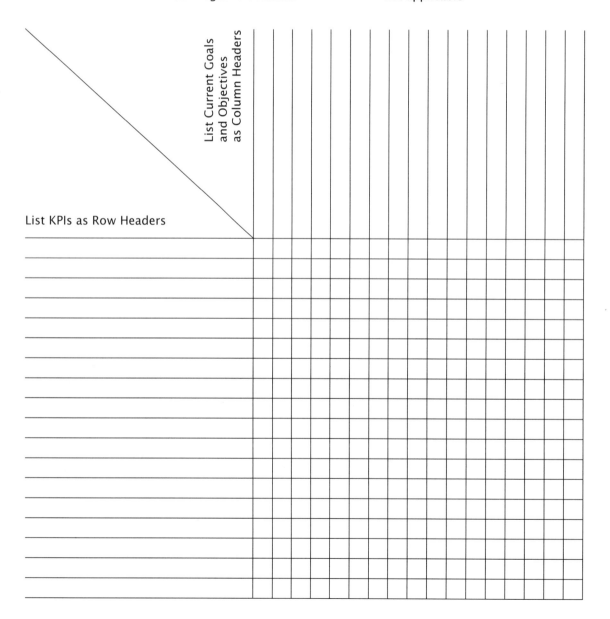

List Current Goals and Objectives as Column Headers

List KPIs as Row Headers

WORKSHEET 3.11   Individual

Cross-Impact Analysis: Organizational Resource Base Effects on KPIs

List the group's final set of excellence areas and high-demand programs and services in the top column spaces and the working list of KPIs in the left hand row spaces. Then indicate in the intersecting spaces what you believe to be the effect of excellence areas and high-demand programs and services on the KPIs. Use the following scale, or use a scale with which the group feels more comfortable.

6 = strong positive influence   2 = moderate negative influence
5 = moderate positive influence   1 = strong negative influence
4 = weak positive influence   0 = neutral, don't know, no impact,
3 = weak negative influence   not applicable

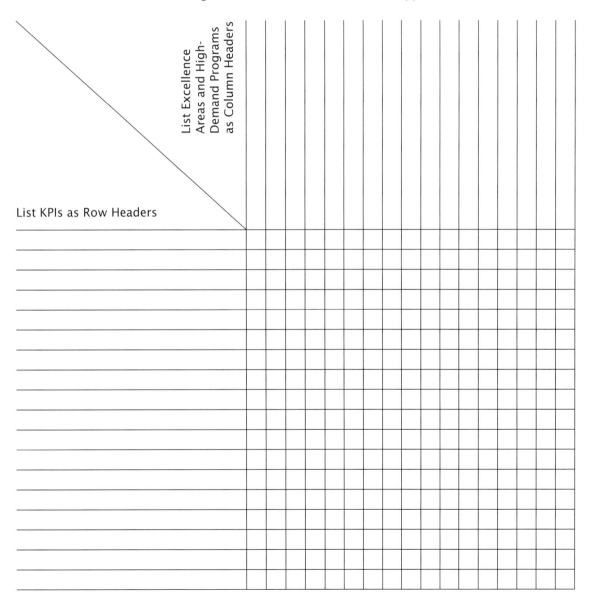

Cross-Impact Analysis: Organizational Resource Base Effects on KPIs (Continued)

List the group's final set of poor-quality areas and low-demand programs and services in the top column spaces and the working list of KPIs in the left-hand name spaces. Then indicate in the intersecting spaces what you believe to be the effect of poor quality areas and low-demand services on the KPIs. Use the following scale, or use a scale with which the group feels more comfortable.

6 = strong positive influence
5 = moderate positive influence
4 = weak positive influence
3 = weak negative influence

2 = moderate negative influence
1 = strong negative influence
0 = neutral, don't know, no impact, not applicable

List Poor-Quality Areas and Low-Demand Programs as Column Headers

List KPIs as Row Headers

WORKSHEET 3.13   Individual

Cross-Impact Analysis: Organizational Resource Base Effects on KPIs (Continued)

List the group's final set of fiscal, capital, and human resource qualities in the top column spaces and the working list of KPIs in the left-hand row spaces. Then indicate in the intersecting space what you believe to be the effect of fiscal, capital, and human resource qualities on the KPI. Use the following scale, or use a scale with which the group feels more comfortable.

6 = strong positive influence   2 = moderate negative influence
5 = moderate positive influence   1 = strong negative influence
4 = weak positive influence   0 = neutral, don't know, no impact,
3 = weak negative influence   not applicable

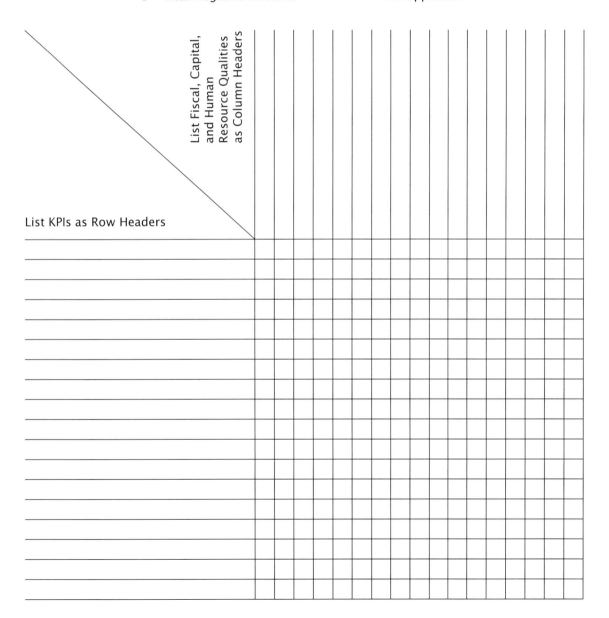

List Fiscal, Capital, and Human Resource Qualities as Column Headers

List KPIs as Row Headers

Listing the Most Important Strengths

Now that your group has conducted the several cross-impact analysis exercises, the SPC should translate the results of the performance, design, and resource base analyses by identifying the most important strengths that the several analyses suggest. Conduct the group exercise using the general rules of brainstorming, as before, and write the top several strengths in the space below. Sort the group choices based on the KPI classification areas. (Strengths are those things that the college or university owns or does that allow it to take advantage of important strategic opportunities.)

Top strengths:

Academic: Campus support:

1.   1.

2.   2.

3.   3.

Enrollments: Information technology:

1.   1.
2.
3.   2.

                                            3.
Administrative:

1.   Other:

2.   1.

3.   2.

                                            3.
Resources:

1.

2.

3.

WORKSHEET 3.15   Group

Listing of Most Important Weaknesses

Again as a result of the several cross-impact analysis exercises your group has conducted, the SPC should now translate the results of the performance, design, and resource base analyses by identifying the most important weaknesses that the several analyses suggest. Conduct the group exercise using the general rules of brainstorming, as before, and write the top several weaknesses in the space below. Sort the group choices based on the KPI classification areas. (Weaknesses are current negative conditions, practices, or deprivations that hold back the college or university from taking full advantage of its important strategic opportunities.)

Chief weaknesses:

Academic:

1.

2.

3.

Enrollments:

1.
2.
3.

Administrative:

1.

2.

3.

Resources:

1.

2.

3.

Campus support:

1.

2.

3.

Information technology:

1.

2.

3.

Other:

1.

2.

3.

Analyzing Strengths, Weaknesses, Opportunities, and Threats

This step is the culmination of the previous three steps. It will help provide a semifinal working list of KPIs, strengths, weaknesses, opportunities, and threats. A lot of data collection will have gone into the many lists that the strategic planning committee (SPC) will have developed in completing the first three steps, and even though the group will already have done a great amount of analysis in determining prioritized KPIs and external and internal environmental factors, this step will take the working lists that the SPC has developed to this point and put them all together. The group will do a cross-impact analysis that measures the combined effects of all of the strengths, weaknesses, opportunities, and threats on the institutional KPIs. The results of this exercise will provide additional information that will allow the group to make some final decisions regarding which of the items in all five lists have interactions significant enough to warrant their continued inclusion in the initial strategic planning process.

The purpose of this step is to measure the impact that each strength, weakness, opportunity, and threat has on the KPIs, as suggested in Table 4.1. The KSWOT cross-impact analysis (KSWOT stands for *K*PIs, *s*trengths, *w*eaknesses, *o*pportunities, and *t*hreats) should be a blind vote with each participant having only a single vote. This method mitigates the potential of opinion leaders disproportionately influencing the vote. The result of this step is a ranked scoring of the external and internal factors that affect an organization's KPIs.

Table 4.1. Sample Individual Cross-Impact Matrix for KSWOT Analysis.

KPIs	Strength 1	Weakness 1	Opportunity 1	Threat 1
FTE enrollment	6	0	3	4
Tuition rate	1	4	5	2
Graduation rate	3	1	0	5
State appropriation	1	1	3	1
Financial aid	2	5	1	3

Outcomes

The normal outcome of the KSWOT cross-impact analysis is one of the first major "ah-ha!" events of the unfolding strategic planning process. What normally happens is that the group as a whole begins to see the interaction effects of the most significant institutional strengths, weaknesses, opportunities, and threats on its essential outcome and health indicators. Patterns tend to become more clear, relationships become more apparent, and the participants begin to develop a sense of how things work together (or perhaps against each other) to affect overall organizational performance. When these outcomes occur, the group has become enlightened in a manner that will help them begin to develop strategies for controlling the environmental forces over the long term. This is the essential first milestone in the strategic planning process.

It is important that the group come to these realizations together. If for some reason one or more of the group members do not see the relationships, it is important for the entire group to discuss how the relationships occur so that each individual comes to the same understanding as the rest of the group. This will be important as the group begins the transition from looking at the conditions that currently exist (Steps 1 through 4) to looking at the conditions that need to develop (Steps 5 through 10).

Hints

1.   Up to the completion of this step, groups may well have a fair amount of skepticism. Thus far, this process may have looked like an exercise in data collection and manipulation. The "ah-ha!" factor that comes to most participants at the end of this step is a transition point for most groups. Most participants tend to lose their skepticism at this stage and begin to focus more on developing

a realistic set of strategies for achieving a positively controlled future for the college or university. Be sure to encourage the "ah-ha!" moment, and even be willing to celebrate it.

2. The matrix for conducting this particular cross-impact analysis will of necessity be quite large. If you have twenty KPIs and thirty-two SWOT items, this means that each person will be making at least 640 decisions. This is time-consuming. But because of the importance of the outcomes of this particular analysis, do not short-cut it. For those doing the paper forms and spreadsheet methods, it is probably useful to send people home to do this matrix, where they can set their own pace and work in a comfortable setting. For those using a decision support center, this analysis should be the last activity of the day, and enough time needs to be provided so that those who work more slowly than others will not feel unnecessarily rushed. When early finishers are done, they can go home so they will not put pressure on those who prefer to take their time.

3. Try to calculate results as quickly as possible and get them to group members as soon as possible. Because this is the culmination of a great amount of effort, people will want to know how things turned out. Schedule the next meeting of the SPC quickly, so that people will be able to discuss the results while the process of obtaining them is still clear in their minds.

4. Though presenting the results represents a major milestone in the planning process, it should not be inferred that additional items can no longer be considered. Our experience has been that this step does help move the group into the next major phase of planning very effectively, but as that planning progresses, holes will appear. The rule must be that as the group develops new information, it should be allowed to act on that information by creating new KPIs and by adding to its lists of strengths, weaknesses, opportunities, and threats.

5. We have also found that some people really dislike this willingness to change what the group has already established. In older methods of planning, such changes and the willingness to change were seen as a weakness of the process. In strategic planning, however, the willingness to change is clearly one of the strengths of the process. It is important for the group facilitator to reinforce that strategic planning is an iterative process and that it *must* change as more information is discovered. Remember, we are trying to control and predict the future to a certain degree, and since these activities are hardly an exact science, the group must be willing to alter its decisions when it is appropriate to do so *in order to keep the planning process relevant* to the future as it unfolds.

Worksheets

Only four worksheets accompany this step. As indicated on the worksheets, each form contains two elements: the KPIs as row headers, and on Worksheets 4.1, 4.2, 4.3, and 4.4 respectively, the strengths, weaknesses, opportunities, and threats as column headers. Those individuals using the paper forms method should fill out each form and turn it in to the facilitator for calculation. Those using the decision support center may do best to combine all four forms into one and then use the matrix tool to calculate the results. This has the advantage of allowing participants to see overall effects by measuring row summaries. Some systems do not have sufficient memory, however, to conduct an analysis on a matrix this large, so doing four separate analyses may be necessary. There are also advantages for those using the spreadsheet method to combining all four forms into a single form and then measuring row (KPI) effects. The instructions for completing the cross-impact analysis may be found in the file "Step4" on the spreadsheet disk. If you would prefer to do each analysis separately, simply redo the cross-impact analysis four times, clearing data each time one of the individual analyses is complete.

WORKSHEET 4.1   Individual

Cross-Impact Analysis: KSWOT Analysis: KPIs and Strengths

Using the group's working list of KPIs and organizational strengths, record the strengths in the top column spaces and the working list of KPIs in the left-hand row spaces. Then indicate in the intersecting spaces what you believe to be the effect of each strength on the KPIs. Use the following scale, or use a scale with which the group feels more comfortable.

6 = strong positive influence   2 = moderate negative influence
5 = moderate positive influence   1 = strong negative influence
4 = weak positive influence   0 = neutral, don't know, no impact,
3 = weak negative influence   not applicable

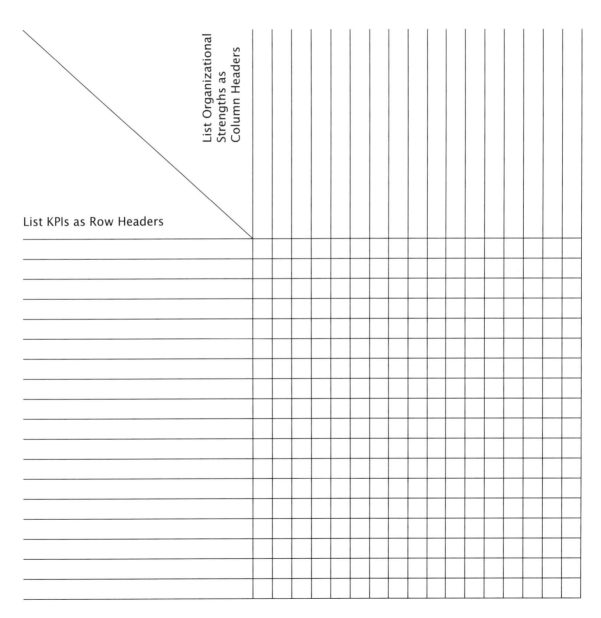

List Organizational Strengths as Column Headers

List KPIs as Row Headers

WORKSHEET 4.2   Individual

Cross-Impact Analysis: KSWOT Analysis: KPIs and Weaknesses

Using the group's working list of KPIs and organizational weaknesses, list the weaknesses in the top column spaces and the working list of KPIs in the left-hand row spaces. Then indicate in the intersecting spaces what you believe to be the effect of each weakness on the KPIs. Use the following scale, or use a scale with which the group feels more comfortable.

6 = strong positive influence   2 = moderate negative influence
5 = moderate positive influence   1 = strong negative influence
4 = weak positive influence   0 = neutral, don't know, no impact,
3 = weak negative influence   not applicable

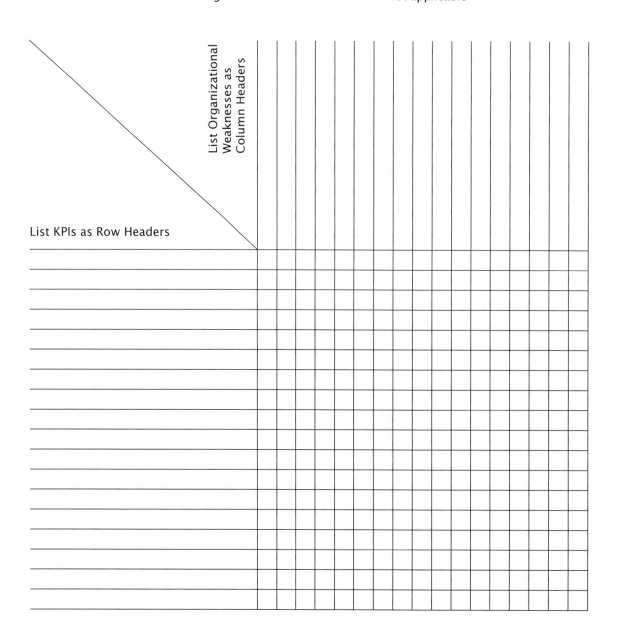

WORKSHEET 4.3 Individual

Cross-Impact Analysis: KSWOT Analysis: KPIs and Opportunities

Using the group's working list of KPIs and organizational opportunities, list the opportunities in the top column spaces and the working list of KPIs in the left-hand row spaces. Then indicate in the intersecting spaces what you believe to be the effect of each opportunity on the KPIs. Use the following scale, or use a scale with which the group feels more comfortable.

6 = strong positive influence
5 = moderate positive influence
4 = weak positive influence
3 = weak negative influence

2 = moderate negative influence
1 = strong negative influence
0 = neutral, don't know, no impact, not applicable

List Organizational Opportunities as Column Headers

List KPIs as Row Headers

Cross-Impact Analysis: KSWOT Analysis: KPIs and Threats

Using the group's working list of KPIs and organizational threats, list the threats in the top column spaces and the working list of KPIs in the left-hand row of spaces. Then indicate in the intersecting spaces what you believe to be the effect of each threat upon each KPI. Use the following scale, or use a scale with which the group feels more comfortable.

6 = strong positive influence   2 = moderate negative influence
5 = moderate positive influence   1 = strong negative influence
4 = weak positive influence   0 = neutral, don't know, no impact,
3 = weak negative influence   not applicable

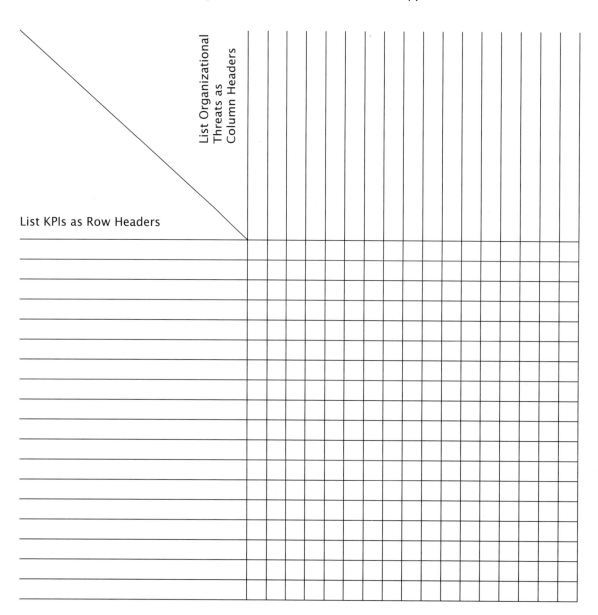

Generating Ideas

As we explained at the end of Step 4, the group is now at a transition point. A lot of work has gone into the development and analysis of data, which has culminated in the KSWOT analysis. Now the question is, What do you do with the results of these analyses? Step 5 asks the members of the strategic planning committee (SPC) to look at the results of its analyses and begin to develop ideas about what the analyses tell it about how the college or university can improve in its most important performance areas. By this time, the SPC should have a fairly strong feeling for which of the KPIs it has developed will stand as the most important for the overall health and well-being of the institution. By solidifying performance in those KPI areas that are already at a high standard, and by improving performance in those KPI areas that are hurting the institution, the SPC will reveal the institution-wide base of strategic planning.

Idea Generation

With a common and focused frame of reference provided by the results of the preceding steps, particularly the cross-impact analysis conducted in Step 4, the SPC is ready to generate ideas. The SPC should use another brainstorming session to solicit ideas on ways to improve the organization's performance as indicated by the KPIs. That is, the SPC members must think of ways to reduce the impacts of threats and weaknesses and to seize opportunities and to enhance strengths. It is important to remember that the ideas that this discussion is to facilitate should be developed according to the rules of brainstorming described in Step 1.

After a review of the results of the Step 4 cross-impact analysis, individuals should first consider how high-performance areas can be maintained, and how those areas in which performance is below expectation can be improved. Then, in the group, each person should contribute his or her ideas one at a time and without comment from other members of the group. The group facilitator should list all of the ideas without comment, and then gather other ideas after the initial input is complete. One important rule continues to apply: *participants must be free to say what they wish without negative comment by anyone else.* Negative comments can seriously reduce the quality and quantity of the ideas. If such comments are heard, the group should move to a blind contribution process. It is also very useful for a permanent record of the ideas to be kept. This will provide a full framework for analysis later. Ideas that do not hold the promise of having the desired impact on the organization's KPIs receive low scores and fall out of contention for implementation.

Ideas generated in this exercise give individuals within the group the opportunity to voice opinions. Again, it is very useful for ideas to be recorded in as complete a way as possible. If ideas initially come out as broad concepts, the SPC will have the opportunity to more carefully define them later. Ideas without sufficient specificity will not make it through the KPI–idea cross-impact analysis.

Expanding on KPIs to Develop a Basic Institutional Strategic Plan

We made a strong argument in our book, and then again early in this workbook, that establishing a practical understanding of the nature of the campus is essential for good comprehensive strategic planning. Until a base is formed by an enlightened view of the institution's internal and external environments, and a broadly accepted institutional vision of itself is established, it is a mistake to move forward in any other aspect of the planning process. On this base, supported by a general agreement on a set of essential KPIs, meaningful strategic planning can proceed.

KPIs play a significant role in determining how various institutional members of the planning process will proceed to build the strategic plan. A comprehensive set of KPIs along with an understanding of the general nature of the institution, its strengths, weaknesses, opportunities, and threats give a remarkably clear picture of where priorities rest. KPIs also identify what elements the institution must consider as it develops its plan and prepares itself to interact with its most critical internal and external environments. KPIs help specify the activities of the campus that the plan must address, where management needs to focus its attention, and where the faculty needs to provide direction, such as in curriculum issues. What all of this suggests is that the strategic plan will lead to new ways of doing things in every part of the campus. And of course this is precisely what the strategic planning process is designed to do.

By focusing on specific areas of performance and institutional health, the strategic plan can be used to develop priorities for management action and for support of academic programs. It can also provide a basis for shifting resources to where they will have the greatest beneficial effect in the long term and to where advantage can be taken of relevant opportunities.

For example, let us assume that undergraduate enrollment survives as a KPI, and the analysis results indicate that institutional strengths such as a nationally known faculty, an above-average technology structure, and a strong endowment base, along with institutional weaknesses such as crowded library facilities, under-enrolled programs in behavioral sciences, and a below-average scholarship pool, all show a strong relationship to this particular KPI. In addition, opportunities such as underserved Hispanic students in the service area and major growth in the service industry, and threats such as competition and increasing governmental regulation and scrutiny, have demonstrated a strong relationship with the KPI. These relationships constitute a set of circumstances that should generate some ideas. One idea might be that by increasing scholarship money (through resource reallocation in the budget) to minority students who are interested in social sciences, enrollments can be strengthened while the institution directly responds to governmental critics who feel the institution has not been active enough in improving its diversity. Another idea might be to seek additional endowments to improve technology in the library, help reduce crowded facilities, and enhance the institution's reputation, which should add additional benefits to student recruiting and retention. Still another idea might be to use the faculty more directly in recruiting students to fill managerial positions in the service industry. Some of these ideas may be good, and others may be marginal or no good at all. That's OK! They are still ideas, and they need to be recognized. Although the third idea just mentioned may be far-fetched on a number of grounds, introducing it to the group might very well lead it to be refined and made into something far more useful to the institution—but this will not happen if the bad idea is not put forward to begin with; then the group is never given the chance to change this proverbial sow's ear into a silk purse.

Outcomes

At the end of this step, the SPC will have identified the areas in which current performance needs to be supported, and those in which it needs to be improved. This knowledge will help justify the activities that the group has gone through to get to this point, and will also be excellent preparation for developing specific goals and strategies to help assure that the institution will be in a position to realize its performance objectives through the strategic planning process. The importance of bringing the strengths and weaknesses into a dynamic relationship with the KPIs should now be more apparent. By tying these elements together, the group will now be in a much more knowledgeable position to take advantage of important opportunities while avoiding major threats that could derail the institution in its pursuit of a more secure future.

Hints

1.   This step requires imagination. Up to this point, the group members have worked with hard data, but now the process asks them to come up with new ideas about relationships with which they are not yet completely comfortable. Be patient, and continuously encourage getting ideas out, regardless of their quality.

2.   The rules of brainstorming must be strictly enforced here, because it is important to get individual participants to develop ideas on their own, even if some of those ideas seem bizarre on the surface. By bringing the ideas into the group consciousness in a nonjudgmental way, the entire group will be rewarded with a wide variety of ideas that will generate invigorating discussion and add life to the process as it continues to build.

3.   Keep to the script. There may be those who will want to jump straight from Step 4 into the development of strategies. This is a mistake. The discussion and activities involved in Step 5 will help cement the understanding of the relationship between the internal and external environment, and of their impact on the college or university's KPIs. The ideas that people bring to this discussion may well become tactics to help implement the strategies that will develop in Step 7.

4.   Encourage additional ideas even after a master list has

been developed. Synergy is a powerful additional dynamic that will help bring additional ideas to the fore and help clarify each person's contribution to the group.

5.   Don't be afraid of the bizarre. Encourage it. It is absolutely true that many seemingly bizarre and ridiculous ideas turn out to be just the type of different and exciting strategies that an institution can use to make a real difference.

Worksheets

There are two types of worksheets in this step. The first type is for use by individuals—Worksheet 5.1. Each member of the group should take time to fill out this form after the group has discussed the results of Step 4 and before it begins its group session to develop ideas. The second type is for group use—Worksheets 5.2 and 5.3—and are to be completed after group discussion about the ideas brought forward by individual participants. Notice that we continue to use the KPIs for developing these worksheets. As individuals and then groups develop their sets of ideas, it will be helpful to keep focused on the categories in which KPIs are grouped. Such a focus will simplify having to come up with ideas for each individual KPI. When the need to develop those ideas comes in Step 7, the SPC will develop strategies that impact groups of KPIs more so than individual KPIs anyway.

Regardless of the method a group is using, all participants should fill out Worksheet 5.1 prior to the group meeting. Those groups using the paper forms method will use Worksheet 5.2 to record the results of their brainstorming prioritization sessions for each KPI area. They will use Worksheet 5.3 to develop a shorthand reference for each of the top prioritized ideas. Groups using the decision support center can use brainstorming programs to gather information, and voting tools to prioritize the data. They can also use the brainstorming programs or idea organization programs to create shorthand references. Groups using the spreadsheet method will find both individual and group spreadsheet templates in the file "Step5" on their disks. These groups can use these templates to gather, prioritize, and create references in a fashion similar to that used by the other groups.

Individual Idea Generation

Prior to the session in which the SPC will develop its list of ideas about how the college or university can support current high-performance areas or realign and improve performance in the areas in which it is not what it should be, individual participants should write out at least four ideas that they believe will strengthen current campus strengths, reduce weaknesses, mitigate threats, and allow the campus to seize opportunities. In preparation for generating these ideas, each person should look over the results of the cross-impact analysis that the group completed in Step 4. Review the examples given above for some suggestions about generating ideas, and then fill in your own ideas under each of the KPI areas indicated below. Please use complete sentences. Be prepared to share your ideas with the group in a brainstorming session, in which you will also be able to add additional ideas that may come as you see what ideas other members of the SPC have generated.

Academic:

1.

2.

3.

4.

5.

WORKSHEET 5.1 *continued*

Enrollments:

     1.

     2.

     3.

     4.

     5.

Administrative:

     1.

     2.

     3.

     4.

     5.

WORKSHEET 5.1   *continued*

Resources (finances, budgets, personnel):

1.

2.

3.

4.

5.

Campus support programs and facilities:

1.

2.

3.

4.

5.

WORKSHEET 5.1

continued

Information technology:

1.

2.

3.

4.

5.

Other:

1.

2.

3.

4.

5.

WORKSHEET 5.2   Group

Group Idea Generation

In this session, the SPC will develop a prioritized list of ideas of how the college or university can support current high performance areas or improve performance in areas in which it is not what it should be. Using brainstorming techniques, each participant is to give one idea at a time as the facilitator lists these ideas together on a black board, display tablet, or something similar until individual lists are exhausted. List ideas in KPI areas, one area at a time. After all individual ideas are listed, the facilitator should ask for any additional ideas. Then the group should discuss the ideas, including any bizarre notions that may have been brought forward, and then prioritize the ideas as described earlier in this workbook. The groups should then select the top five ideas and each individual should list them on this form as indicated below. If the group wishes to list more, it may use the back of this worksheet. Again, please use complete sentences.

Academic:

1.

2.

3.

4.

5.

Enrollments:

1.

2.

3.

4.

5.

Administrative:

1.

2.

3.

4.

5.

WORKSHEET 5.2*continued*

Resources (finances, budgets, personnel):

1.

2.

3.

4.

5.

Campus support programs and facilities:

1.

2.

3.

4.

5.

WORKSHEET 5.2   *continued*

Information technology:

    1.

    2.

    3.

    4.

    5.

Other:

    1.

    2.

    3.

    4.

    5.

Group Idea Generation Shorthand

After the group has selected its tops ideas in each KPI area, it needs to prepare a list to be used in the next step, another cross-impact analysis. To do this, the group should rewrite each idea in a short version using a few key words to represent the larger idea. In the spaces below, rewrite each of the top ideas you have chosen in this shorter version.

Academic:

1.

2.

3.

4.

5.

Enrollments:

1.

2.

3.

4.

5.

Administrative:

1.

2.

3.

4.

5.

Resources (finances, budgets, personnel):

1.

2.

3.

4.

5.

WORKSHEET 5.3   *continued*

Campus support programs and facilities:

     1.

     2.

     3.

     4.

     5.

Information technology:

     1.

     2.

     3.

     4.

     5.

Other:

     1.

     2.

     3.

     4.

     5.

Testing Ideas

This is a short step in comparison with the others the group has already taken, but is an important one because it tests the ideas the strategic planning committee (SPC) generated in Step 5 with the working list of KPIs. The KPI-idea analysis will help demonstrate a group sense of which ideas could have the greatest impact on each of the KPIs. This will be important information for developing goals and strategies in Step 7.

Once the group has generated a set of logical ideas, discussed them, and clarified them, they can evaluate the ideas relative to the KPIs, again through the use of a cross-impact analysis, as shown in Table 6.1. This analysis helps to refine the ideas generated in the brainstorming session and to cluster them into meaningful groups and determine their impact on the KPIs. The SPC must discuss and refine ideas that appear to be without form or specificity so that the group members can assign values from the cross-impact analysis scale. This is another example of self-informing and self-correcting activity. Again, ideas of little or negative impact begin to fall out of serious consideration during this analysis.

Outcomes

The results of this particular cross-impact analysis will demonstrate which of the ideas that the group has developed should be used as a base for building a strategy. It will be important to view the results within KPI areas, to discover trends—that is, clusters of

Table 6.1. Sample Individual Cross-Impact Matrix for KPI Idea Analysis.

KPIs	Idea 1	Idea 2	Idea 3	Idea 4
FTE enrollment	6	5	4	3
Tuition rate	2	1	0	6
Graduation rate	5	4	3	2
State appropriation	1	0	6	5
Financial aid	4	3	2	1

ideas within individual KPI areas, because ultimately a comprehensive strategy may well serve the KPIs in a broad area. For example, if the idea used as an example in Step 5 of increasing scholarship money to minority students through resource reallocation in the budget has constantly generated a strong relationship with several enrollment KPIs, and if the idea of increasing scholarship money to retain top performing students has also demonstrated strong enrollment enhancement relationships, a single strategy of reallocating budget resources to improve scholarships may well emerge. This strategy will have a broad affect on several KPIs and set up several tactical activities as well.

Hints

1. This too will be a rather detailed and time-consuming exercise. Be sure that the cross-impact analysis is conducted at the end of a session, or that it can be done as homework.
2. Be sure that each person understands what this cross-impact analysis is trying to accomplish. Have a group discussion to make sure that everyone is on the same page.

Worksheets

As was true for the cross-impact analysis in Step 4, there are two options in conducting this particular cross-impact analysis. The first option is to do individual cross-impact analyses with the ideas the group has developed in each KPI area and the working list of KPIs. The second option is to do a combined analysis testing of all the KPI area ideas against the working list of KPIs. We would recommend the separate analyses for this step, however, since the SPC will use the results to develop strategies for KPI areas rather than for all KPIs. Nonetheless, no particular harm will come from completing this cross-impact analysis on a combined form, and an advantage may be that it will take a bit less time for SPC members to complete.

As also was true in Step 4, users of the paper forms should use the worksheets printed in this workbook to conduct their analyses and then turn them into the facilitator for computation. If the group wishes to use a single form to complete the analysis, use the grid model found in the forms used for cross-impact analysis to construct a larger form to accomplish this purpose. The groups using the decision support center should use the matrix to conduct their single or several analyses. Finally, those groups using the spreadsheet template method, should use the form in the "CrossImA" file to do one or more analyses, depending on the preference of the group.

Cross-Impact Analysis: Idea Analysis: KPIs and Academic Ideas

Using the group's working list of KPIs and the ideas related to the academic KPI areas, list the academic ideas in the top column spaces and the working list of KPIs in the left-hand row spaces. Then indicate in the intersecting spaces what you believe to be the effect of each academic idea on each KPI. Use the following scale, or use a scale with which the group feels more comfortable.

6 = strong positive influence   2 = moderate negative influence
5 = moderate positive influence   1 = strong negative influence
4 = weak positive influence   0 = neutral, don't know, no impact,
3 = weak negative influence   not applicable

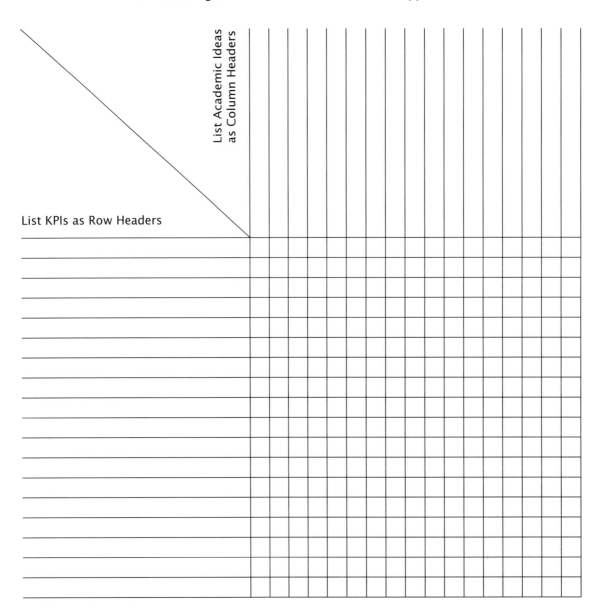

WORKSHEET 6.2   Individual

Cross-Impact Analysis: Idea Analysis: KPIs and Enrollment Ideas

Using the group's working list of KPIs and the ideas related to the enrollment KPI areas, list the enrollment ideas in the top column spaces and the working list of KPIs in the left-hand row spaces. Then indicate in the intersecting spaces what you believe to be the effect of each enrollment idea on each KPI. Use the following scale, or use a scale with which the group feels more comfortable.

6 = strong positive influence   2 = moderate negative influence
5 = moderate positive influence   1 = strong negative influence
4 = weak positive influence   0 = neutral, don't know, no impact,
3 = weak negative influence   not applicable

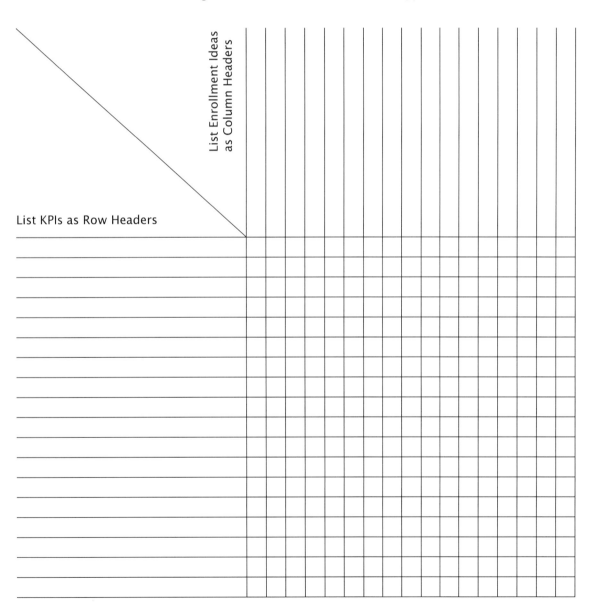

List Enrollment Ideas as Column Headers

List KPIs as Row Headers

WORKSHEET 6.3 Individual

Cross-Impact Analysis: Idea Analysis: KPIs and Administrative Ideas

Using the group's working list of KPIs and the ideas related to the administrative KPI areas, list the administrative ideas in the top column spaces, and the working list of KPIs in the left-hand row spaces. Then indicate in the intersecting spaces what you believe to be the effect of each administrative idea on each KPI. Use the following scale, or use a scale with which the group feels more comfortable.

6 = strong positive influence
5 = moderate positive influence
4 = weak positive influence
3 = weak negative influence

2 = moderate negative influence
1 = strong negative influence
0 = neutral, don't know, no impact, not applicable

List Administrative Ideas as Column Headers

List KPIs as Row Headers

WORKSHEET 6.4 Individual

Cross-Impact Analysis: Idea Analysis: KPIs and Resource Ideas

Using the group's working list of KPIs and the ideas related to the resource KPI areas, list the resource ideas (finance, budgets, personnel) in the top column spaces and the working list of KPIs in the left-hand row spaces. Then indicate in the intersecting spaces what you believe to be the effect of each resource idea on each KPI. Use the following scale, or use a scale with which the group feels more comfortable.

6 = strong positive influence
5 = moderate positive influence
4 = weak positive influence
3 = weak negative influence

2 = moderate negative influence
1 = strong negative influence
0 = neutral, don't know, no impact, not applicable

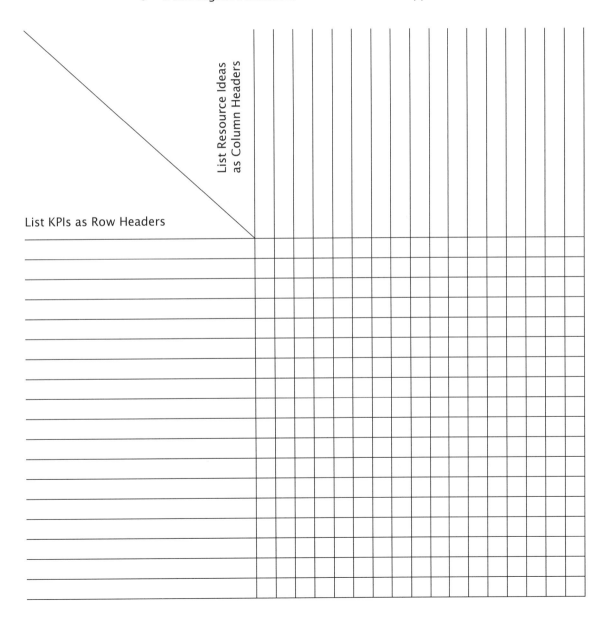

WORKSHEET 6.5   Individual

Cross-Impact Analysis: Idea Analysis: KPIs and Campus Support Ideas

Using the group's working list of KPIs and the ideas related to the campus support KPI areas, list the campus support programs and facilities ideas in the top column spaces and the working list of KPIs in the left-hand row spaces. Then indicate in the intersecting space what you believe to be the effect of each campus support idea on each KPI. Use the following scale, or use a scale with which the group feels more comfortable.

6 = strong positive influence   2 = moderate negative influence
5 = moderate positive influence   1 = strong negative influence
4 = weak positive influence   0 = neutral, don't know, no impact,
3 = weak negative influence   not applicable

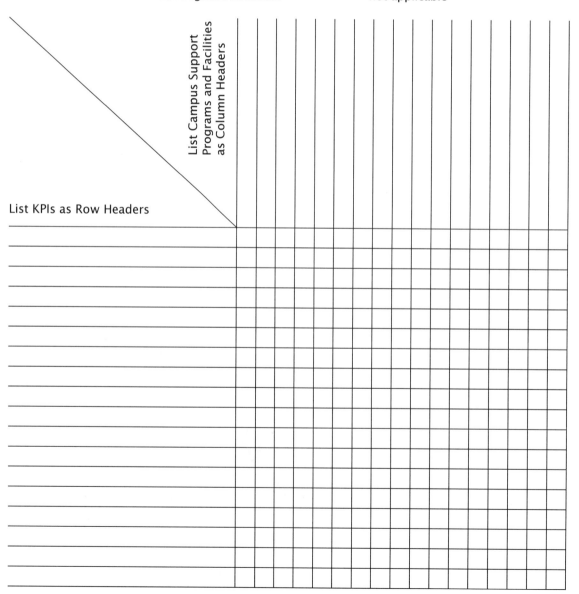

List Campus Support Programs and Facilities as Column Headers

List KPIs as Row Headers

WORKSHEET 6.6   Individual

Cross-Impact Analysis: Idea Analysis: KPIs and Information Technology Ideas

Using the group's working list of KPIs and the ideas related to the information technology KPI areas, list the information technology ideas in the top column spaces and the working list of KPIs in the left-hand row spaces. Then indicate in the intersecting spaces what you believe to be the effect of each information technology idea upon each KPI. Use the following scale, or use a scale with which the group feels more comfortable.

6 = strong positive influence   2 = moderate negative influence
5 = moderate positive influence   1 = strong negative influence
4 = weak positive influence   0 = neutral, don't know, no impact,
3 = weak negative influence   not applicable

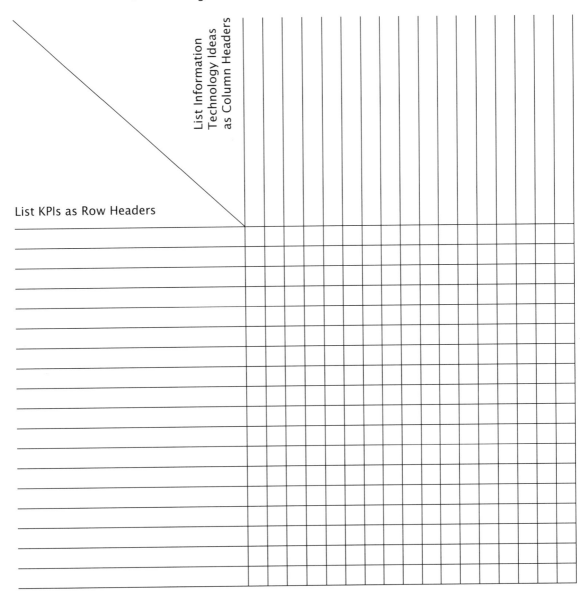

List Information Technology Ideas as Column Headers

List KPIs as Row Headers

Cross-Impact Analysis: Idea Analysis—KPIs and Other Ideas

Using the group's working list of KPIs and the ideas related to the other KPI areas, list the other ideas in the top column spaces and the working list of KPIs in the left-hand row spaces. Then indicate in the intersecting spaces what you believe to be the effect of each other idea on each KPI. Use the following scale, or use a scale with which the group feels more comfortable.

6 = strong positive influence   2 = moderate negative influence
5 = moderate positive influence   1 = strong negative influence
4 = weak positive influence   0 = neutral, don't know, no impact,
3 = weak negative influence   not applicable

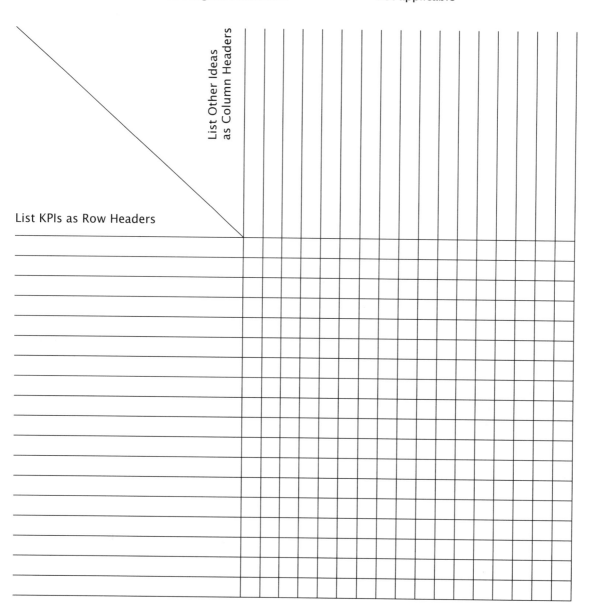

List Other Ideas as Column Headers

List KPIs as Row Headers

Formulating Strategies, Goals, and Objectives

This step signifies the beginning of future-oriented strategic planning. Here is where the strategic planning committee (SPC) will decide what course of action it wishes to pursue and how it will recommend that the college or university proceed. It is worth noting here that all the steps up to this point have prepared a base for doing what most SPC members believed they were involved with strategic planning to do from the very beginning. Some may well have complained that thus far they have not done any planning at all. Well, they are right. What they have been doing is preparing to plan, and all of the work that has gone into the strategic planning process so far has been necessary to help prepare the strategic planners to plan. This step continues to build the KPIs by setting goals and then developing strategies to accomplish them. A final part of this step is to incorporate the institution's (or unit's) mission statement into the plan.

Strategy Formulation

The process of formulating the organization's goals, objectives, strategies, and finally the institutional mission is the culmination of the preceding six steps. Invariably, a discussion arises concerning the definitions of these terms, and it is important to take the time to be sure that all members have the same set of definitions before proceeding to the development of strategies. Notice the positioning of the mission: it comes after all of the other elements of the strategy base are in place. The SPC may now consider it based on a much more solid understanding of who and what the college or university is all about.

With KPI definitions and current measurement secure, with the SPC comfortable with the KSWOT and KPI-ideas analyses, with a common understanding of the purpose for actions the group is about to outline, and with a group expectation about the impact of these actions on organizational performance, the SPC is ready to proceed. The planning group can now begin to write meaningful long-term strategies, and can now cluster ideas into strategies, develop tactics, and assign organizational goals, objectives, and responsibilities.

Defining Strategic Goals

Because the SPC has completed the process of developing definitions and calculating current measurements, it should now develop long-range goals for each KPI. While this process should be as methodical and accurate as possible, it is important to understand that the establishment of goals should not entail inflexible benchmarks. Initial goal-setting exercises may not exhibit high levels of accuracy or quality, due to people's general unfamiliarity with this type of process, and to the fact that available data may not precisely represent a given KPI. So, while it is important to try to establish goals that are realistic and reasonable, in this stage of the strategic planning process, absolutism over goals or how they are set should be avoided. This lack of precision will be overcome in the review process, when the SPC can evaluate progress along the path toward a goal and make decisions about the efficacy of that goal.

Again, some people are uncomfortable developing their goals in this manner. They prefer to set goals up front and then stick doggedly with them. "A goal's a goal!" However, goals are simply attempts to tell the future, and no one can do this precisely. It is important, therefore, from the outset for those involved with strategic planning to realize that goals may change as more and better information becomes available over time. This is not only alright, it is far more realistic than being rigid and will help keep the strategic management process effective over the long term.

Exhibit 7.1 illustrates a case in which the planning group should develop goals in at least two time frames. We recommend that the SPC start with a ten-year goal for each KPI, and then back that up with a reasonable five-year goal. To determine what these goals should be, the SPC members need to talk to those who are now responsible for performance in the appropriate areas (if they are not already a part of the decision-making group) and deter-

Exhibit 7.1.

Examples of Possible Strategies.

Percentage of Out-of-State Students: FTE out-of-state students as a percentage of total FTE enrollment calculated as an average of fall and spring final registration numbers.

Base Year (1992–1993):	19.5 percent
Current Measure (1994–1995):	20.2 percent
Five-Year Goal (1997–1998):	22.0 percent
Ten-Year Goal (2002–2003):	25.0 percent

Strategies: Increase out-of-state recruiting budget by 10 percent the first two years, then by 5 percent the next three years; increase out-of-state scholarships by $30,000 the first two years, then by $15,000 for the next three years.

Percentage of Undergraduate Students Graduating with a Second Language Proficiency: Graduating undergraduate students who can demonstrate proficiency in a second language on standard end-of-second-college-year language exams, as a percentage of all undergraduate students graduating throughout an academic year.

Base Year (1992–1993):	27.6 percent
Current Measure (1994–1995):	29.1 percent
Five-Year Goal (1997–1998):	35.0 percent
Ten-Year Goal (2002–2003):	45.0 percent

Strategies: Make second language proficiency a general requirement for graduation as of the 1999–2000 university catalogue; increase number of foreign language instructors by 10 percent each year until adequate coverage of courses is reached; obtain local business grant to build five new language laboratories.

---

mine what is challenging yet reasonable for each performance area. In the case of KPIs that measure health conditions, such as future state appropriations over which the institution has no direct control, educated guesses based on past trend performance and current information should be used. Again, over time and with better knowledge the SPC will be able to change these goal figures.

Exhibit 7.1 is also an example of a KPI over time. A current measure is presented and the base year (or first year of the planning process) is shown for comparison with the original five- and ten-year goals. This is an example of the control element of the plan, which is described more fully in Step 10, but it is introduced here to demonstrate how control is built into the strategic plan from the beginning.

With these long-term goals in place, the process should be

finished by developing one-year objectives for each KPI. These objectives should be consistent with the five- and ten-year goals, but they will serve as the first major measures of the institution's progress at the end of its first year of implementation.

Initial Strategy Development

Once the planners have established a set of goals that have fairly widespread support, it is time to ask the question, How will we accomplish these goals? The answer requires the identification of specific operational strategies, and begins the process of identifying what specific sets of actions various responsible groups throughout the college or university will need to carry out to achieve the goals.

It is not the intent of the plan to identify highly discrete strategies for the accomplishment of specific KPIs. Rather, as the KPIs are reviewed, it should become apparent that KPIs cluster into sets or categories based on similarities.

Once the SPC has established the type and number of planning area categories it wants to work with it can begin to develop strategies for each category rather than for individual KPIs. This is where the SWOT analysis, done in earlier stages of the process (Steps 2 and 3), comes back into play. The planning group should examine the lists of strengths, weaknesses, opportunities, and threats to determine two things: (1) the relevant opportunities that would help the institution achieve its stated goals in each category, and (2) the capabilities and limitations that will affect the college's or university's ability to take advantage of particular opportunities. The list of threats identifies potential external restraints, and this information helps the planning committee to identify relevant limitations for the various categories involved. Exhibit 7.1 provides two examples of KPIs. Each KPI is followed by a definition that has been agreed upon by the members of the SPC, along with appropriate measures and applicable strategies that the SPC has proposed for achieving performance goals over time.

We are not suggesting "generic strategies," such as those identified by Porter (1980, 1985) for use in the development of business strategic plans. Instead, we suggest that the opportunities that each college and university identifies as plausible for its own particular growth and success are what form strategies. Though each appropriate opportunity needs to be refined into a sustained action plan, it should also be evaluated on its ability to positively impact a specific KPI category and the KPIs within it.

The Mission Statement

One of the central tenets of this method of strategic planning is that while a statement of mission cannot lead the process of strategic planning in colleges and universities, the results of the exercise can lead to a statement of mission. This use of a mission statement better fits the central definition of a mission statement, and a statement developed in such a manner can usefully serve as a formal statement for public consumption of the purpose and direction of the organization. This is important knowledge for those who will be affected by the activities resulting from the implementation of the strategic plan. Mission statements can be helpful in getting people to pull in the same direction in the pursuit of common and well-understood goals.

From the governing board's point of view, the mission statement is the institution's most explicit statement of identity and defines its character. A good mission statement can speak clearly to the concise mission of the institution, describe the types of programs it will offer, state how it will do that, identify the publics it serves, and declare the general societal results that will accrue over the long term. Gone should be phrases such as "a leader in higher education"; these should be replaced with statements such as "national leader in genetic research" or "excellence in teaching to produce the most comprehensively prepared, multidisciplinary, and innovative teachers in the country." These may appear to be risky statements, but if they reflect the strategic direction and purposes that strategic planning has sculpted, then they should appear in the statement of mission.

Properly constructed mission statements can have an important external impact as well (Stott and Walker, 1992). Harrison and St. John (1994) have suggested that mission statements should also address the interests of stakeholders, who can also exert influence. As Brady (1993) suggests, mission statements can serve as a marketing call to arms, because they can express the covenant that exists between the organization and its audience. Such statements may also have important value to several external constituents, including accreditation agencies, who use the stated mission of the institution as a benchmark by which to assess the institution and its management. By waiting to write the mission statement until after the strategic planning process has developed the central constructs of the basic plan, the resulting postanalysis mission statement will be focused and concise, and evident in the strategic choices of the institution. Compared to the generic statements that characterize many college and university mission statements, this is a refreshing difference, and a useful catalyst for strategic improvement of the institution.

To develop a meaningful mission statement, the group should begin by looking at the institution's current mission statement, if it has one. Most colleges and universities do have a mission statement, but those that do not can create one using the rationale provided here.

Examine the current mission statement in light of the KPIs, SWOT items, and strategies the group will have developed by this point. Have a discussion: How does the mission fit the data? How does the mission accurately reflect both the *purpose* and the *direction* the institution will follow as a result of strategic planning? Is the mission statement generic (that is, does it say little more than that the institution will conduct quality research, provide quality education, and engage in meaningful service activities)? Then discuss the following: What should we try to say to our communities about who and what we are? What are the characteristics, qualities, and directions we should capitalize on in a statement of mission? Is there a particular niche we should seek to fill, and is this niche a part of our statement of mission? What, as a result of all the analyses the SPC has conducted, *is* our true purpose and direction? Following these discussions, the group should rewrite (or write) a statement of mission that is much more reflective of the college or university (or unit) than generic mission statements have tended to be.

Outcomes

With the material the SPC has generated in this step it is nearly ready to finalize a plan, present it to the campus communities, and begin the process of implementation. While one final verification step remains in Step 8, certainly the major outcomes of strategic planning are now in place.

Hints

1.   Again, we urge strategic planning committees to be flexible relative to the setting of goals. We realize that the traditional use of goals is much more dogmatic and unbending than we describe it here, and that some people are very uncomfortable working with goals that are subject to change. But this flexibility is

important and is one of the reasons why this form of strategic planning is successful. The willingness to change goals should not be viewed as wishy-washy by either the SPC or the campus. It should be viewed as a strength of the process.

2.   Though strategies will be assigned to individual KPIs, the group should develop strategies in KPI areas, as the worksheet section will indicate. For example, a group may develop three or four strategies for a KPI area, and then find that one or two particular strategies are useful in fulfilling individual KPIs. They may also find that a particular strategy is useful for more than one KPI. For example, increasing scholarship money through resource allocations in the budget (a strategy) may fit under three or four KPIs, and should therefore be listed with them individually, as shown in Exhibit 7.1.

3.   Statements of mission can be issues of great emotion in some groups. While they can serve a purpose when properly conceived and executed, there are other trains of thought that suggest they are essentially useless. Your group has to decide for itself whether or not it should spend a lot of time writing a statement of mission. Since a statement of mission is not a base for planning but rather an outcome of planning, it must derive from the process we have presented in this workbook, and not be used as a rubric upon which the SPC will develop or refine the plan. We understand fully that there are those who disagree with this approach. However, we argue that when the institution bases its plan on achieving a better fit with the environment, it is more important for the college or university to discover what helps it achieve that fit than to risk being out of sync with the environment by going its own way. By going through the process first and then developing a statement of mission, the SPC can provide the institution with a statement that is environmentally considerate, future-oriented, and (it is hoped) creative and exciting.

4.   This step may be among the most time-consuming of the entire process. And certainly the SPC does not want to shortcut anything that it develops here. Be willing to take the time necessary to comprehensively determine goals, consider appropriate strategies, and work on the statement of mission. Schedule enough time to allow the work this step calls for to progress steadily and smoothly. As we have explained, there will be opportunities in the future to correct errors made at this stage, but it is important that the elements of the strategic plan that come from this step be as thoughtfully considered as possible, particularly as communicating these decisions to the rest of the campus becomes more and more of an issue.

Worksheets _____

Most of the work that the SPC will do regarding this step will be done in group discussion and decision making. Those groups that up to this point have used decision support centers or the spreadsheet templates may well find that this particular step (and Step 9) is best done in an open-committee setting, which those using the paper forms methods have used all along. Though the groups that are using decision support centers and the spreadsheet methods can use these facilities to go through this step, they should also be careful to employ as much group discussion as they can to come to group consensus on (1) ten-year and then five-year goals, (2) one-year objectives, (3) strategies for KPI areas, (4) strategy assignments to individual KPIs, and (5) the mission statement. The worksheets included in this step will outline for all three groups a method of going through these various activities.

WORKSHEET 7.1   Group
_____

Ten-Year and Five-Year Goals, and One-Year Objectives

Using the data from Worksheet 1.5, for which the SPC generated a definition and initial measure for each of the KPIs in your working list, update the working list of KPIs (if you have made changes as a result of the several analyses you have performed since Step 1), and then add first ten-year and then five-year goals for each KPI in the appropriate spaces below. Following that, add the appropriate one-year KPI objective as well. The group should add these items after developing additional information from those who are responsible for each area of performance.

Academic:

KPI: _____ Current Measure: _____

Ten-Year Goal _____ Five-Year Goal _____ One-Year Objective _____

KPI: _____ Current Measure: _____

Ten-Year Goal _____ Five-Year Goal _____ One-Year Objective _____

KPI: _____ Current Measure: _____

Ten-Year Goal _____ Five-Year Goal _____ One-Year Objective _____

KPI: _____ Current Measure: _____

Ten-Year Goal _____ Five-Year Goal _____ One-Year Objective _____

KPI: _____ Current Measure: _____

Ten-Year Goal _____ Five-Year Goal _____ One-Year Objective _____

Enrollments:

KPI: _____ Current Measure: _____

Ten-Year Goal _____ Five-Year Goal _____ One-Year Objective _____

KPI: _____ Current Measure: _____

Ten-Year Goal _____ Five-Year Goal _____ One-Year Objective _____

KPI: _____ Current Measure: _____

Ten-Year Goal _____ Five-Year Goal _____ One-Year Objective _____

KPI: _____ Current Measure: _____

Ten-Year Goal _____ Five-Year Goal _____ One-Year Objective _____

WORKSHEET 7.1   *continued*

KPI: _____   Current Measure: _____

Ten-Year Goal _____   Five-Year Goal _____   One-Year Objective _____

Administrative:

KPI: _____   Current Measure: _____

Ten-Year Goal _____   Five-Year Goal _____   One-Year Objective _____

KPI: _____   Current Measure: _____

Ten-Year Goal _____   Five-Year Goal _____   One-Year Objective _____

KPI: _____   Current Measure: _____

Ten-Year Goal _____   Five-Year Goal _____   One-Year Objective _____

KPI: _____   Current Measure: _____

Ten-Year Goal _____   Five-Year Goal _____   One-Year Objective _____

KPI: _____   Current Measure: _____

Ten-Year Goal _____   Five-Year Goal _____   One-Year Objective _____

Resources (finances, budgets, personnel):

KPI: _____   Current Measure: _____

Ten-Year Goal _____   Five-Year Goal _____   One-Year Objective _____

KPI: _____   Current Measure: _____

Ten-Year Goal _____   Five-Year Goal _____   One-Year Objective _____

KPI: _____   Current Measure: _____

Ten-Year Goal _____   Five-Year Goal _____   One-Year Objective _____

KPI: _____   Current Measure: _____

Ten-Year Goal _____   Five-Year Goal _____   One-Year Objective _____

KPI: _____   Current Measure: _____

Ten-Year Goal _____   Five-Year Goal _____   One-Year Objective _____

WORKSHEET 7.1   *continued*

Campus support programs and facilities:

KPI: _____   Current Measure: _____

Ten-Year Goal _____   Five-Year Goal _____   One-Year Objective _____

KPI: _____   Current Measure: _____

Ten-Year Goal _____   Five-Year Goal _____   One-Year Objective _____

KPI: _____   Current Measure: _____

Ten-Year Goal _____   Five-Year Goal _____   One-Year Objective _____

KPI: _____   Current Measure: _____

Ten-Year Goal _____   Five-Year Goal _____   One-Year Objective _____

KPI: _____   Current Measure: _____

Ten-Year Goal _____   Five-Year Goal _____   One-Year Objective _____

Information technology:

KPI: _____   Current Measure: _____

Ten-Year Goal _____   Five-Year Goal _____   One-Year Objective _____

KPI: _____   Current Measure: _____

Ten-Year Goal _____   Five-Year Goal _____   One-Year Objective _____

KPI: _____   Current Measure: _____

Ten-Year Goal _____   Five-Year Goal _____   One-Year Objective _____

KPI: _____   Current Measure: _____

Ten-Year Goal _____   Five-Year Goal _____   One-Year Objective _____

KPI: _____   Current Measure: _____

Ten-Year Goal _____   Five-Year Goal _____   One-Year Objective _____

WORSKHEET 7.1 *continued*

Other:

KPI: _____   Current Measure: _____

Ten-Year Goal _____   Five-Year Goal _____   One-Year Objective _____

KPI: _____   Current Measure: _____

Ten-Year Goal _____   Five-Year Goal _____   One-Year Objective _____

KPI: _____   Current Measure: _____

Ten-Year Goal _____   Five-Year Goal _____   One-Year Objective _____

KPI: _____   Current Measure: _____

Ten-Year Goal _____   Five-Year Goal _____   One-Year Objective _____

KPI: _____   Current Measure: _____

Ten-Year Goal _____   Five-Year Goal _____   One-Year Objective _____

WORKSHEET 7.2   Group

KPI Area Strategies

By making use of the ideas that have come out of Steps 6 and 7, the SPC should identify specific strategies for each of the KPI areas, along the lines presented in the chapter. This may take a fair amount of time, as you consider each KPI area and the several ideas that the group has identified as having an important relationship with the KPIs in each area. So, for example, as you look at the academic KPI area you want to identify several relevant strategies that will impact academic KPIs. Do this for each of the KPI areas. If you wish to develop more or fewer than five strategies in each area, you may do so (use the back of the worksheet to add additional strategies beyond 5).

Academic KPIs:

Strategy 1

Strategy 2

Strategy 3

Strategy 4

Strategy 5

Enrollment KPIs:

Strategy 1

Strategy 2

Strategy 3

WORKSHEET 7.2 *continued*

Strategy 4

Strategy 5

Administrative KPIs:

Strategy 1

Strategy 2

Strategy 3

Strategy 4

Strategy 5

Resources (finances, budget, personnel) KPIs:

Strategy 1

Strategy 2

Strategy 3

WORKSHEET 7.2 *continued*

Strategy 4

Strategy 5

Campus Support Programs and Services KPIs:

Strategy 1

Strategy 2

Strategy 3

Strategy 4

Strategy 5

Information Technology KPIs:

Strategy 1

Strategy 2

Strategy 3

continued

Strategy 4

Strategy 5

Other KPIs:

Strategy 1

Strategy 2

Strategy 3

Strategy 4

Strategy 5

WORKSHEET 7.3   Group

KPI-Strategy Assignments

With the identification of strategies in KPI areas complete, the SPC must now decide which strategies will help achieve the goals identified for each individual KPI. The group should discuss each KPI and the strategies that have been identified for that KPI area and choose one or more strategies from that group that the college or university can use to achieve maximum performance for each individual KPI. Use this form to identify which strategy, or strategies, go with each KPI.

Academic:

    KPI: _____ Strategies:

    KPI: _____ Strategies:

    KPI: _____ Strategies:

    KPI: _____ Strategies:

    KPI: _____ Strategies:

Enrollments:

    KPI: _____ Strategies:

    KPI: _____ Strategies:

    KPI: _____ Strategies:

WORKSHEET 7.3 *continued*

KPI: _____ Strategies:

KPI: _____ Strategies:

Administrative:

KPI: _____ Strategies:

KPI: _____ Strategies:

KPI: _____ Strategies:

KPI: _____ Strategies:

KPI: _____ Strategies:

Resources (finances, budgets, personnel):

KPI: _____ Strategies:

KPI: _____ Strategies:

KPI: _____ Strategies:

WORKSHEET 7.3 *continued*

KPI: _____   Strategies:

KPI: _____   Strategies:

Campus support programs and facilities:

KPI: _____   Strategies:

KPI: _____   Strategies:

KPI: _____   Strategies:

KPI: _____   Strategies:

KPI: _____   Strategies:

Information technology:

KPI: _____   Strategies:

KPI: _____   Strategies:

KPI: _____   Strategies:

WORKSHEET 7.3

continued

KPI: _____   Strategies:

KPI: _____   Strategies:

Other:

KPI: _____   Strategies:

KPI: _____   Strategies:

KPI: _____   Strategies:

KPI: _____   Strategies:

KPI: _____   Strategies:

Statement of Mission

This particular form is a nonform. It provides instructions for conducting a review of the college's or university's current mission (assuming that one exists), poses some discussion questions that the SPC should consider in developing a revised statement of mission (or a new one), and then gives some guidelines for the actual writing of a statement of mission. This particular exercise should be done by the entire group, with the facilitator acting as the chair (the chair offers no opinions, but simply keeps the discussion moving along).

Step 1: Review the current mission statement (when it exists) by asking the following questions (the chair should assign one person to keep notes of this discussion for use when the group begins its work on a new or revised statement of mission):

> How does the mission fit the data?
>
> How does the mission accurately reflect the *purpose* and the *direction* the institution will follow as a result of strategic planning?
>
> Is the mission statement generic (does it say little more than that the institution will conduct quality research, provide quality education, and engage in meaningful service activities)?

Step 2: Discuss as a group the following questions. Your objective is to determine what you want to say in a statement of mission. These questions (and others you may wish to add) will help you focus on what your particular college's or university's mission statement should say.

> What should we try to say to our communities about who and what we are?
>
> What are the characteristics, qualities, and directions we should capitalize on in a statement of mission?
>
> Is there a particular niche we should seek to fill, and is this niche a part of our statement of mission?
>
> As a result of all the analyses the SPC has conducted, what *is* our true purpose and direction?

Step 3: Write a new or revised statement of mission. Put the results of your discussion into words. Be concise and precise. Statements of mission are useful for public consumption, and should tell others what you are, what you do, and what direction you are going. Keep it simple; mission statements that go on and on are seldom useful. Say it in English, avoid "academese." Be bold, dare to state what is important to your college or university, and do not be afraid to identify your niche. Be careful not to construct a mission statement that tries to encompass the activities of an entire campus community, or even its major components—this is not only unnecessary but also reduces objectivity and clarity. The mission statement should define what is unique and distinctive about the campus that helps explain its purpose and direction.

It may be useful to get several of the group's ideas out on the table and then assign a small subgroup to do some "wordsmithing" to put the ideas into a form that the group can then work with. As soon as possible, circulate this draft of the mission statement *to SPC members only* (until you have the mission statement in a more refined form, it is a mistake to share it outside of the central group). Review, revise, and refine. When appropriate, share with others and request their input. Review, revise, and refine again. When the SPC is satisfied, the mission statement may then go out for appropriate approvals.

Determining Institutional Readiness for Change

It is nearly time to formalize the strategic plan by making final decisions on all aspects of it. Before doing so, however, it is important to test the several new items the SPC has developed in Step 7 against the working list of KPIs, to verify that these new items have sufficiently strong relationships with the KPIs to enable the strategic planning committee (SPC) to go forward in developing the finalized plan. The SPC will do this by using the cross-impact analysis one last time to test the goals, objectives, and strategies against the KPIs.

The Goals, Objectives, and Strategies Cross-Impact Analysis

As with the administration of all previous cross-impact analyses, group members vote anonymously and their tallies are aggregated into a composite matrix, based on the model shown in Table 8.1. Once the group knows the final results, it should discuss those cells in the matrix that have large standard deviations to see whether a greater consensus can be reached. Even if full consensus cannot be reached, the group should work to clarify goals, objectives, and strategies to reach a uniform understanding of their definition.

Outcomes

The result of this final cross-impact analysis should provide the SPC with enough assurance about the many items it has selected to

Table 8.1. Sample Individual Cross-Impact Matrix for Strategies, Goals, and Objectives Analysis.

KPIs	Strategy 1	Goal 1.1	Objective 1.1.1	Objective 1.1.2
FTE enrollment	6	5	4	3
Tuition rate	2	1	0	1
Graduation rate	2	3	4	5
State appropriation	6	0	6	5
Financial aid	4	3	2	1

be part of the college's or university's strategic plan that it can then go ahead with the actual writing of a strategic planning document, as outlined in Step 9. If there are any items that clearly do not demonstrate a strong relationship with one or more KPIs, the group should have a discussion about the results to be sure that it can come as close as possible to consensus about an item (although consensus is not imperative). With this high level of agreement, the SPC is in an excellent position to finish up the planning portion of the process.

Hints

1.   Again, this cross-impact analysis may be lengthy. Since there are many details involved, a series of analyses may well be indicated rather than trying to do everything at once.

2.   Since this is the last cross-impact analysis, there may be some apathy from those who have worked hard on the previous analyses and are tired of the process. Try to keep spirits high, and underscore the importance of this particular exercise. By completing this cross-impact analysis and having it verify the relationships the SPC has worked to develop, everyone will be in a much stronger position to complete the plan and communicate it to the rest of the campus.

Worksheets

Two different cross-impact analysis forms are found in this chapter. Worksheet 8.1 is designed to test the several KPI area strategies against the KPIs, and Worksheet 8.2 is designed to test the several goals and objectives against the KPIs. Those groups using the paper forms method can use these worksheets to complete their analyses (note that due to the size of both groups of elements, extra pages have been included). Those groups using the decision support centers will again use the matrix to conduct these two analyses. And finally, those using the spreadsheet templates will use the template for the cross-impact analysis tool found in the file labeled "CrossImA." Instructions for the use of each of these methods are the same as outlined in previous steps.

Cross-Impact Analysis: Strategies–KPIs Verifying Analysis

Using the group's working list of KPIs and the strategies related to the other KPI areas, list the strategies in the top column spaces and the working list of KPIs in the left-hand row spaces. Then indicate in the intersecting spaces what *you* believe to be the effect of each strategy on each KPI. Use the following scale, or use a scale with which the group feels more comfortable.

6 = strong positive influence
5 = moderate positive influence
4 = weak positive influence
3 = weak negative influence

2 = moderate negative influence
1 = strong negative influence
0 = neutral, don't know, no impact, not applicable

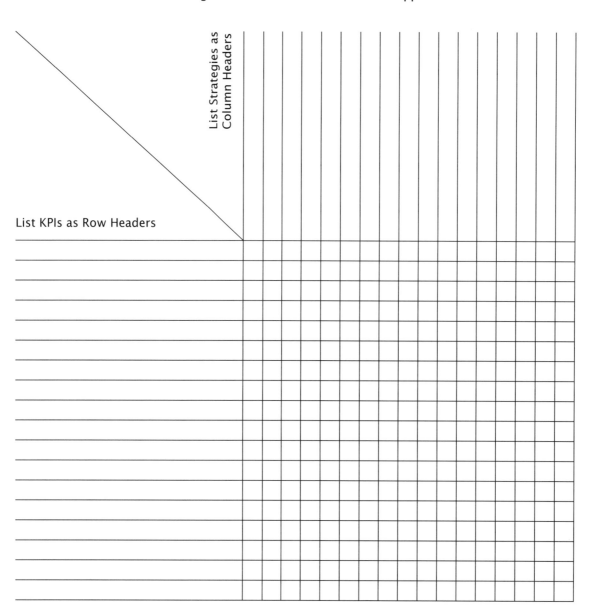

WORKSHEET 8.1

continued

6 = strong positive influence
5 = moderate positive influence
4 = weak positive influence
3 = weak negative influence

2 = moderate negative influence
1 = strong negative influence
0 = neutral, don't know, no impact, not applicable

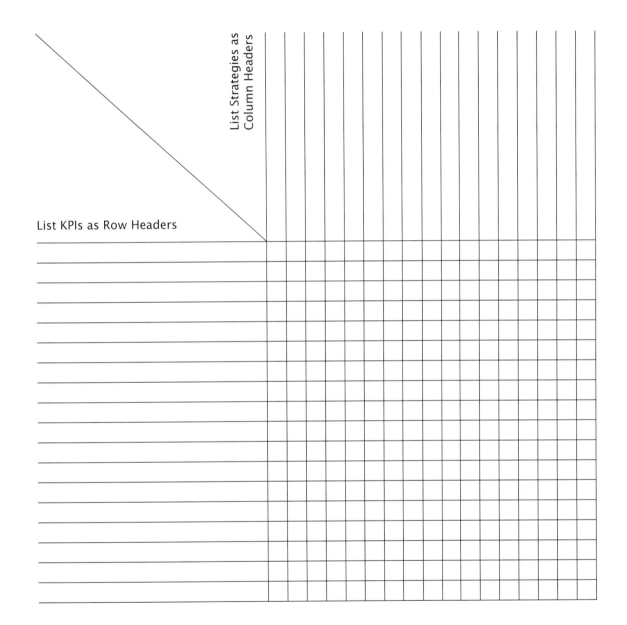

List Strategies as Column Headers

List KPIs as Row Headers

WORKSHEET 8.2   Individual

Cross-Impact Analysis: Goals and Objectives— KPIs Verifying Analysis

Using the group's working list of KPIs and the goals and objectives related to the KPIs, list the goals and objectives in the top column spaces and the working list of KPIs in the left-hand row spaces. Then indicate in the intersecting spaces what you believe to be the effect of each goal and objective on each KPI. Use the following scale, or use a scale with which the group feels more comfortable.

6 = strong positive influence   2 = moderate negative influence
5 = moderate positive influence   1 = strong negative influence
4 = weak positive influence   0 = neutral, don't know, no impact,
3 = weak negative influence   not applicable

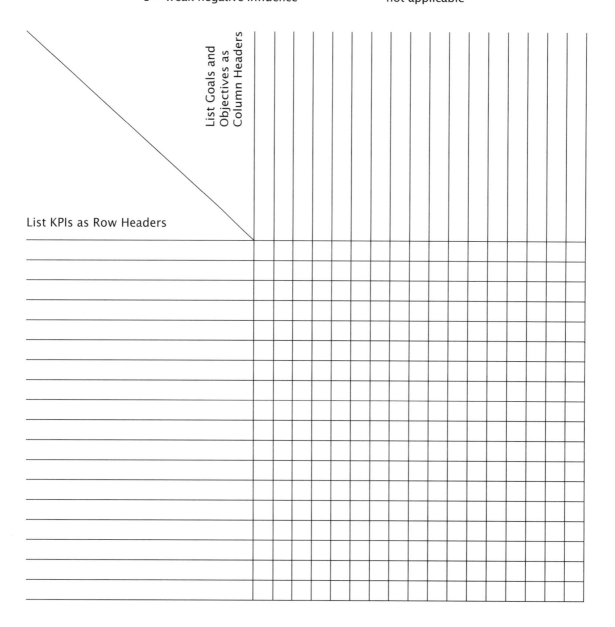

WORKSHEET 8.2

continued

6 = strong positive influence
5 = moderate positive influence
4 = weak positive influence
3 = weak negative influence

2 = moderate negative influence
1 = strong negative influence
0 = neutral, don't know, no impact,
  not applicable

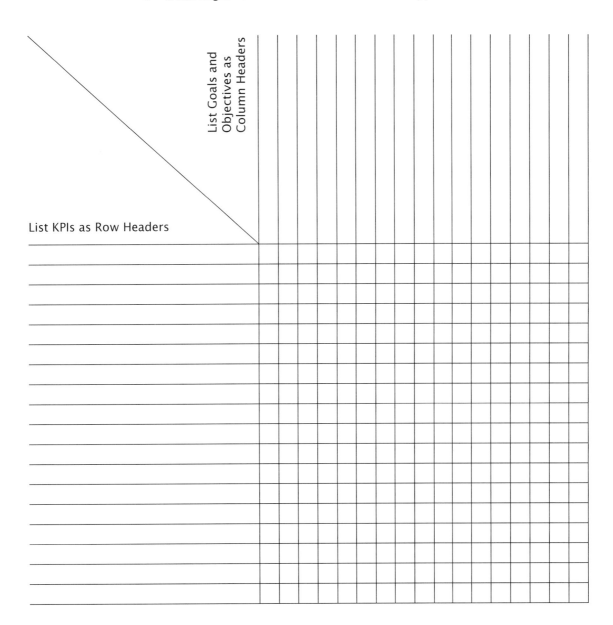

List Goals and Objectives as Column Headers

List KPIs as Row Headers

Implementing the Strategy and Documenting Impacts

This step symbolizes the final step in the strategic planning process. At the end of this step, the strategic planning committee (SPC) will have finalized all of the components of the strategic plan, will have written a document, and will have overseen the implementation of much of the plan. This is not the end of strategic planning, however. With a plan developed and implemented, the work of the SPC is not over. Making sure that the various elements of the plan work as intended requires an appreciable amount of ongoing monitoring and change, as discussed in Step 10. Nonetheless, the completion of Step 9 represents a tremendous accomplishment, and one that should change the nature and direction of the campus significantly over the next several years.

Finalize Strategies, Goals, and Objectives for Implementation

With the final analysis as a guide, the group can fine-tune its decisions and assign them to managers, units, and individual work plans across the campus for implementation. As part of this implementation, the SPC must give responsibility to specific operating units to maintain the information required to monitor progress according to the KPIs. Although these responsibilities may be spread throughout the organization, we recommend that a centralized support unit, such as an institutional research office, be given both a facilitating and a coordinating role in assembling KPI results in a systematic fashion.

In practice, the application of the strategic planning engine must be tailored to each specific setting. The nature of individual colleges or universities, particular sets of opportunities and challenges, the history of planning on particular campuses, and the quality of campus leadership all affect the customization of the strategic planning engine. This tailoring affects the composition of the SPC, the balance between different parts of the strategic planning engine, and the nature of the KPIs, strategies, and goals that result.

The physical outline of the plan should be fairly simple, as follows:

Title page

Table of contents and preface

Introduction

> Brief description of the institution

> Concise environmental analysis

Explanation of the planning model (brief)

KPIs within defined planning areas (with definitions, measurement methods, current measure, initial measure, five-year goal, ten-year goal, and critical issues associated with the KPI)

Explanations should be kept to a minimum and the section dealing with KPIs should be done in outline form. The result will be that the entire document will be easily readable, and those who go through it will be able to determine easily the major tenets of the plan. The section on strategies does require a fairly substantive discussion as to how the proposed strategies will impact performance in the KPI areas, but with some careful editing, the writer or writers of this section can keep it to relatively few pages. The result will be a document that a broader range of people will be likely to read and one that the strategic planning committee will be able to change easily, particularly if the document is always kept in draft form.

Illustrative of these principles, one of the authors, who served as the strategic planner at the University of Northern Colorado (UNC), updated the plan and redistributed it approximately every three to four months. At UNC, the plan was not professionally printed, which allowed for quick turnaround of new plans and rapid dissemination to members of the campus community.

Implementation

Implementation of various segments of the strategic plan often occurs while other parts of the plan are still being developed. For example, once the SPC has determined that the college or university needs to focus its recruiting efforts on attracting more minority students, and once it has developed and approved relevant goals and strategies, those who appropriately develop policy in this area can approve this part of the plan and put it into action. In other words, it is not necessary to have a completed plan in place in order to approve parts of it. Once approved, that part of the plan can be immediately implemented by those who have responsibilities in the appropriate area.

This is essentially the scheme in which all parts of the strategic plan will be implemented. It is important that those people who are responsible for performance in the areas the plan has identified as most important (the KPI areas) should have some say in and input into the portion of the plan that affects them. This way, when the plan takes shape and appropriate approvals are sought, those who have the responsibility for those areas will be ready to implement at once.

Campuswide votes or approvals by a college or university governing board may also be part of the expected process. If these eventualities are possible, it is obviously important to keep the campus and/or the governing board informed about the progress the SPC is making toward the final planning document, and individual campuses must be sensitive from the outset to the routes toward approval, as we explain in detail in our book.

Outcomes

The major result of the completion of this step will be the formal planning document. That is the only visible outcome from a process that will have created many other outcomes. What the process will also be responsible for is a change in the way managers, faculty leaders, and the governing board view the day-to-day management and operation of the campus. As a result of the planning process, everyone on campus should be more fully aware of the place of the university within a defined set of environments. This result should also lead to long-range thinking and decision making that can bring a strategic focus to the campus that it has not witnessed before. If the overall process has been effective, there should be a new sense of *institution* across the campus, in which people are at least more aware of the central goals and direction of the college or university, and at most more actively involved in helping make sure that the institution is accurately aligned with its most important internal and external environments.

Hints

1.   Begin this step by reviewing the results of the final cross-impact analysis. Make sure that the entire SPC reviews the results and comes to an agreement as to what the results indicate. If more work is needed in one or more areas, complete that work before proceeding with this step.

2.   Do not write a long, involved document. Follow the outline presented earlier, and resist the temptation to add data tables that have resulted from the SPC's many data lists and analyses. Limit the document to the working facts—brief explanations about the process, lists of the KPIs with their measures and goals, and descriptions of how the college or university will implement its strategies. It is possible to keep the document to between ten and twenty pages, and the shorter the document the better.

3.   When the document is completed, celebrate your accomplishments! A lot of dedicated people have worked hard to develop the strategic plan, and it is a good idea to recognize these efforts in some way, whether with a dinner, a reception, or some other token of appreciation. These people will now be ambassadors to the campus and beyond, and it is important to let them know in some formal fashion that the college or university appreciates their efforts.

4.   It may be helpful to conduct this step in at least three different sessions. The first session should concentrate on what should go into the plan, and on appointing one or more subgroups to "wordsmith" the document itself. The second meeting should be held after the subgroups have prepared their portion of the document for the entire SPC to review. One individual can take the results of this discussion and combine everything into a semifinal document. The third meeting can then review the semifinal document, make whatever revisions are appropriate, and agree on a finalized document.

Worksheets

Rather than develop specific worksheets on which to write the college's or university's strategic plan, we have developed an exercise to help walk SPC members through the writing, review, and finalizing of the strategic planning document. Regardless of the method groups have used up to this point to develop the plan, all groups should go through the exercise we outline here to prepare their strategic planning document.

Writing the Strategic Planning Document

Using the outline we introduced in the text portion of this step, the SPC can readily put together a strategic planning document that accurately reflects the central tenets of the strategic plan and presents it in a manner that will be easy to read and assimilate across the campus (and beyond). Here we provide some additional information as to what each part of the report should contain.

Title page

The title page should contain the name of the document and the institution. We also urge that the word "draft" or something similar be added to indicate that the plan will always be "in progress."

Table of contents and preface

The next page should contain the table of contents, the same as any formal report, to be followed by a preface that outlines why the college or university has gone through a strategic planning exercise, who was involved, who authorized the process, and what the SPC believes it has accomplished. The revised mission statement fits well into this portion of the report and can be added at the end of the preface.

Introduction

This portion of the report needs to describe what the SPC focused on as it developed the strategic plan. It should contain a brief description of the institution and a concise environmental analysis. As mentioned elsewhere, these descriptions should be kept brief. Talking about what the current nature of the institution is, is more effective than giving a history. Also, by describing in broad terms how the SPC has come to understand its environmental set, this narrative can inform readers about the important relationships that exist between the college or university and its more important environmental constituencies. These relationships are the basic reason for doing strategic planning.

Explanation of the planning model (brief)

This part of the report should describe what the SPC did in developing the plan, without going into details such as the results of the several cross-impact analyses.

KPIs within defined planning areas

This is perhaps the most important part of the report. Here the SPC will outline its working set of KPIs, categorized in KPI areas. Each KPI should include its working definition, an explanation of how its outcomes will be measured, the current measure, the initial measure (if this is not the initial report), a five-year goal, a ten-year goal, a one-year objective, and the strategies associated with the KPI (here strategies should only be named, not explained—that comes in

WORKSHEET 9.1 *continued*

the final part of the report). It is important to keep this part of the report simple in presentation (see examples in the text found throughout this workbook) and low on explanation.

Strategies

This final part of the report will be the most narrative. Here the SPC should describe each of the strategies it has introduced in the discussion of KPIs and explain how the college or university will use them to continue current high-level performance or to enhance performance in those areas in which it needs to improve. Again, although more explanation is needed here, work to keep the explanations as clear and simple as possible.

And that's it. You have completed your document, and you are ready to celebrate a job well done. Your job isn't finished just yet, however. Be sure to stick around for Step 10.

Evaluating and Revising the Plan

As we have argued in our book, strategic planning should lead to strategic management. Once the plan is written and its tenets are implemented, it is important to make sure it works. This can only be done by maintaining some form of the SPC and having it review progress over time. This step describes the activities that the successor SPC should carry out periodically to assure that the plan is working as it was intended to, or to make changes in the plan (remember, the document should always be a draft, so that it can be easily updated when updating is appropriate).

Monitor and Evaluate Strategies, Goals, and Objectives

Toward the end of the first year of living under the plan, particularly if precise measurement methods have been identified and are in use, the SPC will have better information available to it than when it implemented the plan, and this information will help sharpen goals and strategies. The campus should view this process as the maturing of the plan rather than as an indication that strategic planning is not working. If planners and the people they communicate with across the campus will keep in mind that strategic planning is a long-term process, then patience should soothe the campus and help everyone recognize that the process is constantly self-improving.

Table 10.1. Quarterly Evaluation of Strategies, Goals, and Objectives.

Strategies, Goals, Objectives	Q1	Q2	Q3	Q4
Strategy 1 (5 to 10 years)	O	D	D	O
Goal 1.1 (3 to 5 years)	O	D	O	O
Objective 1.1.1 (1 year)	O	D	O	C
Objective 1.1.2 (1 year)	O	O	C	C
Goal 1.2 (3 to 5 years)	D	D	D	O
Objective 1.2.1 (1 year)	O	O	O	C
Objective 1.2.2 (1 year)	C	C	C	C
Objective 1.2.3 (1 year)	D	D	D	X
Strategy 2 (5 to 10 years)	O	O	O	O
Goal 2.1 (3 to 5 years)	O	O	O	O
Objective 2.1.1 (1 year)	O	O	O	C
Objective 2.1.2 (1 year)	O	C	C	C
Goal 3.1 (3 to 5 years)	O	O	O	D
Objective 3.1.1 (1 year)	O	O	O	D
Legend: O=On Track/ D=Delayed/ C=Completed/ X=Abandoned				

Perhaps the most useful tool in the strategic planning engine is the formal process of evaluating the institution's strategies, goals, and objective. As the college or university implements its various planning components, it usually finds it enlightening to measure performance on a periodic basis. Annual reviews are very important, but reviews that occur more often help the campus management keep in control of activities and have a direct impact on the long-term results. Table 10.1 presents a frequently used review form, based on quarterly reviews. Such a form enables an organization to track its progress toward achieving its strategies, goals, and objectives. If performance falls in line with expectations, then the SPC can conclude that it has chosen appropriate strategies. If performance falls outside of expectations, then the SPC must ask hard questions about its strategies, goals, and objectives and be willing to make adjustments that more realistically address the KPIs, SWOTs, goals, objectives, and strategies set in place to help guide the campus toward a successful future.

Outcomes

Follow-up is essential for an effective strategic planning and strategic management process. Each element of the KPIs must be updated periodically (at least once a year, though two or four times a year is better), and the best group to do this update is the individuals on the SPC who created the original plan. As we suggested earlier, the ongoing SPC may well be a fraction of the original SPC (depending, of course, on the size of the original group). But it is important for the successor SPC to continue its monitoring activities, as suggested in this step, and to make adjustments, additions, and deletions to the original plan and then make these changes known to the appropriate areas of the campus. If this is done on an ongoing basis, the SPC will ensure that the plan will be effective in the long-run, and that has been the point all along.

Hints

1. At the end of Step 9 and before the SPC disbands, make sure that the successor SPC is appointed and that the meeting times are set for the next twelve months (twenty-four months is even better.)

2. Membership in the successor SPC may be different than the original SPC, if the committee desires, and may include major campus administrators and faculty leaders to make sure that those people who are in charge of implementing the plan are tied into the review process.

A Final Word

Strategic planning, as we have described it here, is a process that can be beneficial to any college or university, regardless of its circumstances. At the same time, strategic planning is not a process that happens by osmosis. It is a continuum of interactions, investigations, analyses, decisions, and actions that must come together in a coherent and coordinated manner. This workbook has developed this process from the viewpoint of the steps that must be in place if strategic planning is to be effective and to develop a coherent and logical position from which the campus can proceed toward achieving rewarding, inspired, and environmentally friendly goals. We believe that when a college or university chooses to follow the model we present here, and does so in a dedicated fashion, the results will be positive and effective.

However, there is another concern that we need to highlight. It is a crucial mistake to forget that the strategic planning process involves people who represent ideas, traditions, passions, and political persuasions. In other words, a set of forms to fill out and a model to follow does not entirely explain how the process will work on any given campus. Furthermore, each college or university is unique in many ways. While this uniqueness is one of the things that strategic planning hopes to identify and build on, the strategic planners must also tailor the model to fit the people and circumstances present on each campus. This may well require outside assistance, and each SPC must weigh the task before it and decide whether a consultant may be useful to help do the tailoring required. Some campuses may decide this is necessary, while others may not. Regardless, the bottom line must be the creation of an effective and efficient process that will objectively examine the campus and its environment, critically analyze and evaluate the resulting data, and creatively and uniquely fashion a strategic plan that will work. The future of the institution may well be at stake.

We wish you and your campus the best of luck in following the guidelines we have presented in this workbook. We believe that your campus will be better prepared for the future by doing so, and you will have served the campus well by helping to position it to achieve a better fit with its environment—an environment that will only become more and more complex and invasive as we move into the future world of higher education.

Worksheets

The next page contains a model for a worksheet that we suggest the SPC might develop and use on an ongoing basis to conduct scheduled, periodic reviews of the strategic plan. Of course each particular SPC should expand this basic model to fit the precise number of KPIs, goals, and objectives that are in that particular college's or university's strategic plan. A similar template is also available for those using the spreadsheet template method. This template may also be expanded to match the precise number of items the SPC will want to monitor and control.

Periodic Review of the Strategic Plan

The SPC that will follow the progress of the college or university strategic plan should meet on a regularly scheduled basis to review progress made on all KPIs, goals, and objectives. Using the form provided here as a model, construct a matrix that identifies the KPIs, goals, and objectives. Fill in the appropriate spaces to identify the KPIs, and enter the goals and objectives under "measures." Finally, add the current measure of the objective and include the date of the measurement. If this evaluation is done quarterly, the SPC will report its decision regarding the status of each KPI in the status boxes under Time 1, Time 2, and so on. Time 1 is the first quarterly decision, Time 2 is the second quarterly decision, and so forth. This single worksheet will work for four different review sessions, unless major changes are made that precipitate a new evaluation sheet for the next review session.

KPIs, Goals, Objectives	Measures	Time 1	Time 2	Time 3	Time 4
KPI 1:					
Goal 1.1a (10 years from the base)					
Goal 1.1b (5 years from the base)					
Objective 1.1.1 (1 year)					
Date: *Current Measure*					
Objective 1.1.2 (1 year)					
Date: *Current Measure*					
Goal 1.2a (10 years from the base)					
Goal 1.2b (5 years from the base)					
Objective 1.2.1 (1 year)					
Date: *Current Measure*					
Objective 1.2.2 (1 year)					
Date: *Current Measure*					
Legend: O=On Track/ D=Delayed/ C=Completed/ X=Abandoned					

REFERENCES

Brady, J. "The Search for Mission Control." *Folio,* 1993, *22,* 42, 51.

Dolence, M. G., and Norris, D. M. "Using Key Performance Indicators to Drive Strategic Decision Making." In M. H. Borden and T. W. Banta (eds.), *Using Performance Indicators to Guide Strategic Decision Making.* New Directions for Institutional Research, no. 82. San Francisco: Jossey-Bass, 1994.

Harrison, J. S., and St. John, C. H. *Strategic Management of Organizations and Stakeholders.* St. Paul, Minn.: West, 1994.

Porter, M. E. *Competitive Strategy.* New York: Free Press, 1980.

Porter, M. E. *Competitive Advantage.* New York: Free Press, 1985.

Rowley, D. J., Lujan, H. D., and Dolence, M. G. *Strategic Change in Colleges and Universities: Planning to Survive and Prosper.* San Francisco: Jossey-Bass, 1997.

Stott, K., and Walker, A. "The Nature and Use of Mission Statements in Singaporean Schools." *Educational Management and Administration,* 1992, *20*(1), 49–57.

INDEX

Disk Order Form

Those groups that are interested in using the spreadsheet method of conducting the strategic planning process we describe in this workbook may order disks that contain the spreadsheet templates. The disks are available directly from the authors at the address below. Please note the disks and programs that are available. Do not order disks for versions of spreadsheets older than the ones we list. We apologize in advance if we cannot provide you with a template set that matches your particular spreadsheet, and we hope you will be able to use one of the other methods of conducting the strategic planning process.

To order, please fill in the blanks below and mail this entire form to the address provided, along with your check in U.S. dollars (no credit card orders please) in the appropriate amount.

Name: _____

College or University: _____

Address: _____

City: _____ State: _____ Zip Code: _____

Daytime Telephone: _____

No. of Disks	Program for:	Price per Disk	Total
_____	Excel for IBM, Version 6.0 or higher	$15.00	_____
_____	Lotus 1–2–3 for IBM, Version 3.0 or higher	$15.00	_____
_____	Quattro Pro for IBM, Version 6.0 or higher	$15.00	_____
_____	Excel for Mac, Version 4.0 or higher	$15.00	_____
		Subtotal	_____
		Shipping and handling, $2.00 per disk	_____
		Colorado residents add 3 percent sales tax	_____
		Total	_____

Mail this form and your check to:

Dr. Daniel James Rowley
Department of Management
College of Business Administration
University of Northern Colorado
Greeley, Colorado 80639